My Beloved

Powerful and Prophetic –
God's Abundant Grace for Your Life

Colin Urquhart

Marshall Pickering
An Imprint of HarperCollins*Publishers*

Marshall Pickering is an imprint of
HarperCollins*Religious*
part of HarperCollins*Publishers*
77–85 Fulham Palace Road, London W6 8JB
www.christian-publishing.com

First published in Great Britain
in 2000 by Marshall Pickering

1 3 5 7 9 10 8 6 4 2

Scripture quotations are taken from the *Holy Bible,
New International Version*, © 1973, 1978, 1984
by International Bible Society. Used by permission
of Hodder & Stoughton Ltd, a member of
the Hodder Headline Plc Group. All rights reserved.
'NIV' is a trademark of International Bible Society.
UK trademark number 1448790.

A catalogue record for this book is
available from the British Library.

ISBN 0 551 03263 4

Printed and bound in Great Britain by
Omnia Books Ltd, Glasgow

To all those who long
to know God better
and to live in a deeper and closer relationship
with Him

Contents

Acknowledgements

First and foremost, I am so thankful to the Lord for the amazing grace He has shown me during the fifty years I have known Him, and the thirty-seven years of my ministry. Absolutely all the glory belongs to Him.

At the human level, I am thankful to God for my wife, Caroline, for her love and support, together with all the members of my family who I rejoice to say all serve the Lord with us at Kingdom Faith.

I also want to thank all the team and members of Kingdom Faith Church for their wonderful love and encouragement. God has blessed us so richly with a people of great love and faith, whose hearts are set on living the contents of this book.

In particular, I want to thank my personal assistant, Paula, not only for her work on the book but for fielding all the other aspects of the administration involved in my ministry, especially when I am writing.

My thanks also to Lara for her long hours at the computer, and to Lisa who helped in the early stages.

Last, and by no means least, my thanks to Elizabeth and her team for their hidden ministry of upholding me in prayer while writing this book. May the Lord use it for His glory!

A Word of Explanation

Ten years ago, *My Dear Child* was published. Little did I antici-
pate then the amazing response this book would produce, or the
many thousands of copies that would be sold.

Writing this book, a series of prophetic words given me by the
Lord, proved to be a life-changing experience for me. Reading it
proved to be a life-changing experience for many people. The
book encouraged people in their faith, strengthened them in
their personal relationship with God as their Father, and helped
them to become attuned to the voice of God themselves.

Because of the initial response to *My Dear Child*, the sequel,
My Dear Son, was published a year later. Written in a similar
style, it gave readers personal revelation of Jesus Christ and was
again well received.

Before I began writing the first of these books, the Lord spoke
to me about writing three books in this style. Here is the third:
My Beloved.

Although written in the same style, God speaking to His
beloved child, it covers different subject matter from the
previous books. It speaks of the way God expresses His love
through His grace and shows the reader how to live in a close
walk with God through Jesus Christ, living by faith in His grace.

As with the previous books, I have drawn aside to be with the
Lord, to listen to His 'heart-beat', to seek to bring to your heart
something from His own heart.

Like all prophetic literature, there has to be an element of
humanity in what is written here. It has been my practice for
nearly forty years to spend time daily with the Lord, writing down

what I believe He has said to me by His Spirit. These times have been wonderful and have been a vital strength to me over the years, enabling me to become increasingly sensitive to His voice.

I certainly do not claim any infallibility here. However, I do believe you will hear God speaking to you personally in what is written; and that is the important thing as far as I am concerned. I trust that *My Beloved* will help you to become more attuned to the voice of God's Spirit: to know that He wants to speak to you daily to encourage you in your faith.

HOW TO USE THIS BOOK

The 80 sections of this book will take you through a progressive revelation of how the life of Jesus Christ can be expressed more fully in your life as a believer. It is intended that one section should be used daily and in a prayerful manner, so that you apply the principles outlined in your personal life. This will greatly encourage your faith as you see more clearly what Jesus has done for you and how, through the Holy Spirit, you can live in His love and power.

This material has had a profound effect on the lives of those associated with Kingdom Faith Ministries, who are enjoying a move of God as an outworking of His grace enabling us to live as His beloved children.

Understand that each section of this book is addressed to you personally as one of God's beloved children. Receive what is written as a personal word to you. See how the message is then confirmed through the scriptural references given at the end of each section.

You will find this encouraging for your faith and relationship with the Lord. You will also find that He will speak to you in a similar fashion; that you will be able to write down what you believe He says to you in His wonderful grace and love.

Colin Urquhart

I Have Loved You

'I have loved you,' says the LORD.
Malachi 1:2

My beloved! Yes, you really are my beloved child. I have already shown my love for you, not simply in words but through all I have done for you. Would I have sent my Son to die for you unless I loved you? Such sacrificial love cannot be equalled, and certainly doesn't depend on your circumstances or feelings. This is sacrificial love in action!

Each one of my children can say that Jesus died for them. This doesn't make His death any less personal, for I had *you* in mind when I sent Jesus to give His life on the cross. I know this is difficult for you to understand; nevertheless, it is the truth: When Jesus died on the cross you were personally involved.

Who else has loved you so much? Who else has died in your place? The death He died was the death you deserved because you have sinned against me and have grieved me. He suffered *your* punishment.

In any system of justice lawless people have to be punished. To me, sin is lawlessness; it contravenes my divine law and therefore my will. I couldn't say that sin doesn't matter, for it separates people from me, excluding them from heaven. Yet because I love you so much I had no desire to punish you. I wanted to reveal my love to you, to make you one with me, your holy Father, able to inherit my Kingdom. Now you can live free from punishment as a child of my grace.

I have not only dealt with the consequences of your sinful past, but want to give you the very best I have, my own life. This is even more difficult for you to believe, isn't it? You deserve punishment but I give you life instead! You see, it is my nature to love, and no loving father wants to punish his children; he desires to give them the best he has.

Because you accepted that Jesus died for you, that He suffered the punishment you deserved for your sins, you only had to turn to me and ask me to forgive you for everything in your life that has grieved me. I forgave you, took away your sins and set you free from guilt. I will never hold those sins against you; they are gone for ever.

No longer do you need to be ashamed before me. Is it asking too much of you to believe this? Your unbelief is due to the fact that you have never encountered such love before. But I cannot reduce the level of my love for you. I forgive you completely, because it is my nature to be merciful; this means my treatment of you is the very opposite to what you deserve!

Of course, it grieves me if you return to those sins I have forgiven. You can be thankful that my mercies are new every morning, and that every time you turn back to me I am always ready to forgive you. However, if you truly love me you will not abuse this mercy by having a casual attitude towards sin. It cost me the death of my Son, so I never think lightly about it.

My desire is to see you walking in my way, free from sin and able to enjoy the fullness of my life that Jesus came to give you.

John 3:16   Isaiah 53:5   1 John 1:9

I Have Redeemed You

Fear not, for I have redeemed you;
I have summoned you by name; you are mine.
Isaiah 43:1

My beloved, do you understand what it means for me to say I have redeemed you? I was prepared to sacrifice my Son so that you could become my beloved child. I gave His life for yours! With the shedding of His blood He paid the necessary price so you could belong to me.

You see, beloved, it is not only my nature to love and be merciful; I am also holy and righteous. I want my children to know my love and mercy; but I want them also to be like me, a holy and righteous people.

All sin is unholy and unrighteous. Before you could become my child, therefore, all your sin had to be forgiven, washed out of your life so that you could be clean before me. This is not some impossible dream; it is what Jesus has already done for you. He *has* redeemed you. He *has* paid the price so you are now mine. He *has* purchased you for me! And the price was the shedding of His blood. Yes, beloved, that is how much I had to pay to make you mine.

My beloved, I know you by name. Your personal relationship with me began when you were born again, when you asked me to forgive your sins and you put your faith in Jesus, in what He did for you on the cross.

At that time it seemed to you that you were making a momentous decision, to humble yourself and ask for my forgiveness. And so you were. Yet you took that step in response to my call. My own Spirit had begun to work in your heart to show you your need of forgiveness, to make it clear that you could only be rid of your guilt and find true peace by turning to me. So, whether you realized it or not, you were responding to my initiative.

I chose you because I wanted you to become my beloved child, the object of my love and blessing. **So when you gave your life to me, I gave my life to you**. That was a wonderful exchange, wasn't it? You gave me your life, with all your sin, failure and inadequacy; and I gave you my life, eternal life, full of love, joy and power. I didn't force that life upon you; I waited until you wanted me to give myself to you.

I am your *gracious* Father; you are a child of my grace. I gave you the fullness of my life, even though you deserved nothing from me. **I called you by name, forgave you your sins, made it possible for you to belong to me for ever, and gave you my life**.

My love is not expressed in sentimental feelings but in positive action, in the works of my grace, **giving everything to those who deserve nothing**. Yes, I know whom I have chosen. I know you, every thought, desire and intention. I know your struggles; I know you see so many things about yourself that are unholy and unrighteous, and that you wonder why I should have chosen you and question how I could possibly love you!

When I forgave all your sins I cleansed you of all unrighteousness through the holy blood Jesus shed for you. Unless I had regarded you as holy and righteous in my sight, I could not have given you my own life, eternal life. As it is, I have loved you by making you a child of my grace, my own dear child whom **I love, care and provide for**. I demonstrated that I had accepted you by giving you everything although you deserve nothing.

You are truly my beloved!

Ephesians 1:4   Romans 3:22–24   John 5:24

3

My Precious Child

Since you are precious and honoured
in my sight, and because I love you ...
Isaiah 43:4

My beloved, you are precious to me. You estimate the value of your possessions by how much you paid for them: I do likewise. So think of the price I paid for you! The life of my Son, Jesus! Can you understand how precious you are to me, therefore, that I should be prepared to pay such a price for you?

You look after highly valued possessions; so do I! **Because you are mine, I care for you and seek your best interests.**

Yes, you are honoured that I have called and chosen you to be my beloved child. There is no greater honour for anyone to receive. This is a much higher honour than that given by the world to its superstars in sport, entertainment or business. You are honoured by God, not man. I honour you now, and I will honour you in heaven after you have proved faithful in your love for me.

Even when things are not right in your life, I don't stop loving you. You are not any less precious to me because you have sinned and failed in some way. I remain with you always, and at such times seek to restore you to my will.

If I loved my children only when they obeyed me perfectly, I would have a very small family on earth! As it is, there are millions like you. I know each by name, every one is precious to me and I live in each one to bring them to the fulfilment of the destiny that I have for them.

Because you have received my Holy Spirit, you are among the most favoured people on earth. Truly honoured! The Creator of heaven and earth has chosen you for His child, has become your Father and placed His own Spirit within you.

Because you are so precious to me, I want to be precious to you, your most treasured possession. Yes, I am *your* God, *your* Father, and my own Spirit lives in you to enable you to honour me. How privileged you are!

What did I have in mind when I called you? I wanted to free you from all the consequences of your sin and selfishness, and give you a sense of direction and purpose. Sin is never my will for any of my children; it cuts across my purpose for them. Now you are my beloved child you can discover my true purpose for your life. Why waste your life by drifting from one month to another without any sense of direction, not knowing the plans I have for you?

I don't want you to reach the end of your life on earth thankful for all I have done for you, yet without accomplishing the purpose I had for you. My beloved, you are not only a child of grace; you are also a child of destiny! And it is I who have chosen your destiny for you.

However, you have to understand that my purpose for you cannot be fulfilled unless you receive what I desire to give you. I have not called you to work for me, but for Jesus to live in you so He can work through you. What He does through you will be far more effective than anything you could do for me. You are natural; His life within you is supernatural.

Romans 8:28   Ephesians 1:11   Philippians 2:13

Full of Grace and Truth

The Word became flesh and made his dwelling among us.
We have seen his glory, the glory of the One and Only,
who came from the Father, full of grace and truth.
John 1:14

I sent Jesus from heaven, full of grace and truth. I had given my law to my people through Moses; but grace and truth came through Jesus Christ. Under the law, my blessings were available to those who obeyed. Through the gospel Jesus taught, my blessings are made available to those who believe in my grace.

Jesus came with the truth of my heavenly Kingdom and made it possible for people to receive the life, authority and blessings of my Kingdom *now*. They don't have to wait until they go to heaven to participate in those riches. I intend them to begin the process of receiving their inheritance as soon as they believe in Jesus and become part of my Kingdom on earth. This certainly is the work of my grace, for how could anybody earn or deserve such an inheritance, now or in heaven?

Jesus is the truth. Understand that truth is not a series of concepts, but is embodied in the person of Jesus Himself. He came to earth full of truth and His words are eternal truth, conveying my life to you and to all who put their trust in Him.

Jesus came also full of grace. He gave to people despite their unworthiness. My grace was worked in and through Him as He freely gave to people, healing them, setting them free from bondage and meeting their needs.

When they came to be healed, people didn't try to impress Jesus with the things they had done or with their own righteousness. They knew they didn't deserve to be healed or receive a miracle from Him. Neither did Jesus question them about their past. He only wanted to know if they expected to receive their healing from Him. Did they believe He would graciously meet their need?

Jesus showed my grace to His disciples in other ways as well, forgiving them for their lack of understanding and slowness to believe despite the great things they witnessed.

Beloved, because Jesus is the same yesterday, today and for ever, He is always full of grace and truth. From the fullness of His grace you are able to receive blessing upon blessing, as did those first disciples.

I am willing to give today and will never come to the end of my giving to you. The more you believe in my grace, the more I will be able to give into your life; and the more you will then be able to give to others. Yes, you will be a blessing because of all you receive through my grace!

I express my grace in what I give in practical ways, and I give abundantly, generously.

It is true that I want you to obey whatever I ask of you. Yet my grace doesn't depend on your obedience, but on my willingness to give. When you expect me to be gracious my blessings are released into your life.

I know you think you should be doing something for me, rather than me doing something for you. Such thinking shows a lack of understanding of my grace. What can you do for me? You even need my grace to enable you to obey my word; you can never please me by the things you do in your own strength. My gifts depend on my grace, not on your effort!

John 1:7   Luke 12:32   Romans 5:17

Grace and Faith: The Power Connection

For it is by grace you have been saved, through faith –
and this not from yourselves, it is the gift of God –
not by works, so that no one can boast.
Ephesians 2:8–9

My beloved, I have done everything necessary for the salvation of all humankind through the death and resurrection of Jesus. Although it is my will for all to be saved, *only those who put their faith in this work of my grace shall be saved.* Without faith it is impossible to please me, for it is only by faith that the forgiveness and new life I have made available can be received. Without faith my purposes for my people cannot be accomplished.

My grace didn't begin the moment you first believed; all the blessings of my grace were already awaiting you. They only became yours, though, when you first believed. But you have not yet appropriated all I have made available to you through Jesus. I want faith to become a way of life for you, so there can be a continual flow of my grace in your experience.

Faith and grace are like the two wires necessary to make a connection of electrical power. If you connect the positive wire without connecting the negative, you don't make a power connection. And if you connect the negative without the positive, you still don't make a power connection. To release the power, you need to connect both wires.

Faith and grace work together. When faith is placed in my grace it makes the power connection, and you see a release of my life and activity in the circumstances of your life.

You see, my beloved, faith is not a matter of you trying to make me do something I don't want to do or give you something I don't want to give. Faith enables you to take hold of all the blessings of my grace that are waiting to be appropriated by you.

There is no other way to obtain them: you will never deserve them, nor can you earn them.

Do you consider your faith weak and inadequate? Listen, beloved, faith is a choice. You can choose to believe either what I say or something that contradicts what I say – something you think yourself, or that someone else has said to you, or even what the enemy wants you to believe. When you read my word, you have to choose whether you believe what I say or not. **To live by faith in me is to make the right choices.**

Look at the ministry of Jesus. The people who made the right choices were healed, delivered, set free and received my life. You would not have described some of them as religious or knowledgeable, or people with dynamic lifestyles. There were outcasts, prostitutes, beggars and misfits among them. But they made the right choices; they chose to believe what Jesus said and could do.

Yes, some of them were desperate. If they had not chosen to trust Jesus they would have died and been destroyed by their problems. He made clear to them that their faith, simple and desperate though it was, had saved and healed them.

Who made the wrong choices? Who chose to reject Jesus and what He said? Many of the religious leaders, who chose to believe their religious traditions were more important than Jesus' words. Those traditions, He said, nullified His words and robbed them of the life they could have received.

It is so important for you to know from my word what I have done for you and made available to you through my grace. Those words of truth are as powerful today as when they were first spoken or written. **My beloved, lay hold of the inheritance that is yours through my grace. Believe what I say and don't doubt my word. Make the right choices! You are who I say you are. You have what I say you have. You can do what I say you can do – through my grace.**

Matthew 19:25–26   Acts 2:21   Romans 5:9–10

Salvation through Grace

Therefore, since we have been justified through faith,
we have peace with God through our Lord Jesus Christ,
through whom we have gained access by faith into this grace
in which we now stand.
Romans 5:1–2

My beloved, it is important for you to know that you are accepted, isn't it? In particular you want to be sure I have accepted you, especially because there are many occasions when you feel unworthy and totally unacceptable to me or to anyone else! The good news is that your acceptance doesn't depend on how you feel, or on what you have done. It is dependent totally on what my Son has done for you.

I am righteous; everything I do is right. I want my people to be righteous, to be in right standing with me, and to do what is right in my eyes. It was impossible for anyone to achieve right-eousness, to be brought into right relationship with me, through their own works. No matter how hard you try there is nothing you can do to make yourself acceptable to me. What is the point of trying to do this, when you only have to believe what Jesus has done for you to be made acceptable? I cannot accept you through anything you have done; only through what He has done! Now you believe in Him, you are accepted 'in the Beloved'.

You see, beloved, your acceptance is not in yourself, but in Him. Once you realize this you can be at peace instead of condemning yourself every time you fail.

Such a righteousness could only be made possible as a gift of my grace. **Faith in my grace is all that is necessary to make a person righteous**. That person is then justified, made totally acceptable in my sight, not through anything they have done but through faith in the work of the cross. Jesus literally took upon

Himself all that makes you unrighteous and unacceptable. When He died, that unacceptable person you used to be died with Him. Now you believe in Him, you are a new creation, righteous and acceptable to me.

Paul explains this: 'This righteousness from God comes through faith in Christ Jesus to all who believe' (Romans 3:22). Then, in the next breath, he affirms that those who believe 'are justified freely by his grace through the redemption that came by Christ Jesus' (v. 24). So grace and faith belong together.

This same principle is true of all my dealings with my children. I want my children to continue to live in the righteousness that is theirs through my grace. I want them to enjoy my salvation that is theirs through my grace. I want them to live the saved life, living in the continuing revelation of my love and my desire to do them good. I want them to walk in the good things I have prepared for them.

I want Paul's personal testimony to be your testimony:

> *I have been crucified with Christ and I no longer live, but Christ lives in me. The life I live in the body, I live by faith in the Son of God, who loved me and gave himself for me. I do not set aside the grace of God, for if righteousness could be gained through the law, Christ died for nothing.*

> Galatians 2:20–21

I have given you the gift of righteousness through faith in Jesus Christ. This is a work of sheer grace on my part. You could not have done anything to deserve this, and certainly you could do nothing to earn such acceptance. Jesus' righteousness has become your righteousness through faith in my grace. So you don't have to strive to accomplish a righteousness of your own. That would be impossible anyway. For centuries people have tried to do this and failed. You don't have to achieve what Jesus has already done for you!

I have taken hold of your life and placed you and all believers in Christ, so that now His life has become your life.

He came and completely identified with you in your need, so that now you can be completely identified with Him in His heavenly life. I don't see you separate from Him, unacceptable because of sin, weakness and failure. I see you living in Him, cleansed by His blood and justified, made righteous and totally acceptable to me. It is essential that you understand that this complete identification of yourself with Jesus has taken place. His righteousness has become your righteousness, His holiness your holiness; His life is now the life you can live and enjoy. All this is the work of my grace. You can do nothing except believe what I have done for you.

Romans 1:17   Romans 3:21–22   Galatians 2:21

7

That You Might Become Rich

For you know the grace of our Lord Jesus Christ, that though
he was rich, yet for your sakes he became poor, so that you
through his poverty might become rich.
2 Corinthians 8:9

Beloved child, you wonder how you can be completely identified with Jesus. It is simple! Though Jesus was rich, yet for your sake He became poor, so that you through His poverty might become rich. He had to leave the glory of heaven, and became poor by accepting the limitations of humanity. He identified totally with your condition and your need.

I sent my Son to share in the poverty of human existence, to be tempted in every way, to experience the weakness you know only too well. The wonderful truth is that in all things He remained faithful to me and fulfilled completely the task I had given Him.

Understand my motive in sending Jesus. It wasn't to make Him poor, *but to make you rich*. That is the measure of my grace. In order to make you rich with all the blessings of my grace, He had to be made poor. There was no other way to realize my objective. So when He came, Jesus took on Himself all the sins and transgressions of my people. He was bruised, He was crushed, rejected, scorned, reviled, hated, and ultimately suffered the death penalty of the guilty, although innocent Himself.

The sight of Him hanging on the cross, experiencing separation from me for the only time in His existence, was the ultimate expression of poverty. But look at the riches that are yours as a result of this work of grace – the riches that belong to you and to all who acknowledge Jesus as their Lord and Saviour!

- **You have been born again by my Spirit**. He lives in you to enable you to live in my grace.
- **You have been given the fullness of my life**, eternal life, God's life!
- **You now belong to my Kingdom**, and the life of that Kingdom has been placed within you.
- **You have become a new creation**. The old person you once were, a sinner separated from me, is dead, buried and finished with, crucified with Christ. Now you are a new creation, able to live in my grace.
- **You have been placed in Christ**, so that you are not only my child but a co-heir with Him.

All this is the measure of my grace. You are already my child; already a co-heir with Christ. I have already blessed you in Him with every spiritual blessing in heavenly places. These are the riches He came to give you.

And what did you do to accomplish any of this? Absolutely nothing! You could do nothing to make yourself my child; nothing to give yourself eternal life or make yourself a co-heir with Christ. You could do nothing to make yourself a new creation. You were powerless to do anything to achieve the fullness of Christ's life that I have given you.

Yet by putting your trust in Jesus, all these gifts become yours! This was totally the work of my grace, for you could never deserve or earn an eternal inheritance in heaven that can never perish, spoil or fade, but that is kept for you. **Through my grace you have been made rich.**

Therefore, my beloved, I want you to live in the good of these riches that are yours in Christ. Unbelief in my word will rob you, for you cannot live in the good of riches you don't believe you possess. By faith you can appropriate all that I have made available to you through my grace.

Jesus took upon Himself all that makes you poor, so that through His poverty you may be made rich. Enjoy my grace; don't deny it!

Don't misunderstand the poverty of Jesus. He was never in need, because I provided everything for Him. Neither did He exalt poverty. To me, poverty is a curse that I want to see removed from the lives of my people. As Paul put it, Jesus 'became a curse' through dying on the cross to remove that and every other curse that can afflict my people.

Beloved child, I don't want you to live under any curse, but in the full flow of my blessings made available to you through my grace, for in Christ you have been made rich. This is not you wanting to be rich; it is your God and Father telling you that you are rich!

Romans 5:1–2   Hebrews 11:6a   Romans 11:6

8

Seated in Heavenly Places

And God raised us up with Christ and seated us
with him in the heavenly realms in Christ Jesus.
Ephesians 2:6

Beloved, does it seem incredible to you that you have been made rich? You are more wealthy than you realize! When you first put your faith in Jesus, I did two amazing things for you. I put you into Him and I put His Spirit into you.

Jesus came to share your humanity so that *now* you can share His heavenly life. You were in Him when He died on the cross. When He died, you died. The person you once were, the sinner who could do nothing to please me, was put to death. In Christ you were raised to a new life and became a new creation. Because He overcame death, you too will overcome death.

The Holy Spirit, whom I have placed in you, is the power by which Jesus was raised from the dead. Yes, beloved, that same power is living in you and can work through you. This power not only strengthens you in your natural life, but is my supernatural power that transcends your natural life, the power that will work for you as well as in you.

You were in Christ when He returned to the glory of heaven. There He reigns far above any ruler, or authority, or power, or leader, or anything else either in heaven or on earth. You are there in Him, seated in heavenly places, in the place of victory. I don't see this as some future event, but as a present reality: **you are in Him NOW, seated in victory with Him NOW. Because He has overcome, you are able to overcome in Him NOW.**

Does all this seem unreal to you? This is only because you don't see yourself as I see you: in Christ, completely identified with Him, one with Him. Once you accept this truth you realize the immense potential you have. **You have His life because you**

are in Him and He is in you. This is why Jesus told His disciples to abide in Him and He would abide in them. They were to live in the continual awareness of their unity with Him and their ability, therefore, to make His life their own.

Does it surprise you that I have chosen you to be a disciple, that I have given you the same privileges? Jesus taught the disciples that apart from Him they could do nothing. But if they continued to live in Him and He in them, there was no limit to what He could do through them.

Beloved, the same is true for you. You cannot do apart from Him what can only be done in Him. You cannot accomplish with your natural abilities what can only be achieved through His supernatural power and grace. This is why I stress your need to live by faith. Believe that I have placed you in Christ, so that His supernatural life is now your life. **Your initial act of faith led to you being placed in Christ. Your life of faith enables you to live in Him, availing yourself of all the supernatural resources and blessings that are yours in Him.**

When you try to fulfil my purpose with your natural abilities you fail, no matter how hard you try. This is because my will for your life can only be accomplished through that risen, supernatural power of Jesus Christ. Because you are in Him and He is in you, that life and power is already available to you. You are raised along with Christ and seated with Him in heavenly realms – far above every ruler, authority and power on earth. If you allow Him to reign in your life, you will be able to exercise the authority of my Kingdom over the enemy and every spiritual power that opposes you.

This is further evidence of my grace. Beloved, even if you find it difficult to understand how such great things could be true for you, you can still choose to believe them. You can trust the revelation of my word and thank me for all that I have done for you. **I have placed you in Christ, raised you in Him, and seated you in heavenly places in Him.** I believe it, and I should know!

Of course, your physical resurrection has not yet taken place. What I am impressing on you is that **you live in the risen, reigning Christ by my gracious act, and so His victorious, all-conquering life is yours.**

I want to teach you how to live in Jesus, where I have placed you, and allow His supernatural power to work for you. That power can accomplish in your life infinitely more than you could ever accomplish yourself.

Why should I have done something so wonderful as to place you in the risen, triumphant, reigning Christ? To show the incomparable riches of my grace expressed in my kindness to you.

Romans 5:17   Ephesians 1:3–6   Ephesians 1:7

Enriched in Every Way

For in him you have been enriched in every way –
in all your speaking and in all your knowledge.
1 Corinthians 1:5

My beloved, it is a supreme act of grace on my part that I have taken hold of you and placed you in my Son, Jesus. **In Him you have been enriched in every way.**

I know you don't always feel as if you are in Christ. The truth is not what you feel, but what I say and what I have done for you through Jesus. The truth is that because I have placed you in Christ you have been enriched in every way; not will be enriched, in the future, but you have already been enriched in every way in Him.

How can you be sure that you live in Christ, in God? There are two simple tests. Do you acknowledge that Jesus is my Son? If so, you live in me and I in you. Have you received my Holy Spirit? His presence within you is proof that you live in me and I in you. Well then, the matter is settled: you live in me and I live in you. You live in Christ Jesus and He lives in you.

Now you can rely on the love I have for you. I want you to continue to live in Jesus, to be rooted and built up in Him, strengthened in the faith I am teaching you, and overflowing with thankfulness. I keep impressing on you that my love for you doesn't depend on how you feel, but on what I've done for you.

You have all the riches of my life as your own. What a great privilege! Of course, such a privilege brings certain responsibilities. **You are to live a life worthy of your calling.** There is little point in thanking me that I have placed you in Christ while living as someone who is outside Christ! You can only live in Him by becoming deeply rooted in my word.

Remember, Jesus is the Word of God. To live in Him is to believe His words and allow them to live in you. You can't enjoy your inheritance if you don't believe what He says! So choose to accept what He teaches; His words have much greater authority than your thoughts or understanding. Humbly accept that, as you live in Him, His life can be revealed through you.

Do you notice how often Jesus healed the sick, cast out demons, raised the dead and performed such miracles as the calming of the sea simply by speaking a few words? This demonstrates how powerful His words are; they are filled with divine life. He speaks and sins are forgiven, lives are changed and miracles occur.

His words are as powerful today when you believe them, and just as true. They are still filled with life, His life that has the power to transform your life. This is true also of the words He spoke through His apostles; they are words of truth and life.

So, beloved, because you are in Christ you have been enriched in every way. Speak what is true over your life. Don't contradict what I say about you. As you read the New Testament it can become an exciting adventure to discover the nature of the life you have in Christ.

Colossians 3.3   1 Corinthians 15:57   2 Corinthians 2:14

The Fullness of My Grace

*From the fullness of his grace we have all
received one blessing after another.*
John 1:16

My beloved, you can live in the continual revelation of my grace, of my willingness to give to you, *irrespective of anything you do or deserve*. The mistake many of my children make is to think that my grace is extended to them in order for them to be saved from their past life and the power of the enemy; but that then subsequent blessings are somehow dependent on a combination of my grace and their works. Nothing could be farther from the truth.

Didn't Jesus say that even when you have done everything you should, you are still unprofitable servants? What does this mean? That all your works do not profit you. **I don't bless you according to what you have done, but according to what Jesus has done for you**. You will certainly receive much more by depending on what He has done rather than your own efforts! I have given you all the blessings and benefits that go with salvation; they are the riches that are already yours in Christ. Jesus constantly drew upon these heavenly resources while on earth, and He taught His disciples to do likewise.

Why pray as if you are uncertain whether I will answer or not? Don't imagine that I am fickle, deciding to bless some believers and not others. **I have given to every one of my children the same inheritance, the same position and the same life in Christ.** If Jesus died to make all the blessings of my grace available to you, I certainly want you to avail yourself of those blessings. I will not see His sacrifice wasted!

I *want* to give to you. So pray with confidence in my faithfulness, that I will surely fulfil my promises to you as my child. When you ask, believe you have received your answer because you are laying hold of what I have already chosen to give you as your inheritance in Christ.

Don't keep looking at yourself, wondering if you have been good enough to deserve the answer you need. Stop that introspective self-condemnation that robs you of faith and confidence when you pray. If I only gave to you when every detail of your life was in perfect order, I would not answer by grace, but as a reward for your goodness. And you can never be good enough to deserve anything; such thinking is a denial of my grace. As with those who came to Jesus, there is one thing I want to know: **are you trusting in my grace to give to you even though you deserve nothing?**

Ephesians 1:13   Colossians 2:10   Ephesians 4:1

All Grace Abounds to You

And God is able to make all grace abound to you, so that in
all things at all times, having all that you need, you will
abound in every good work.
2 Corinthians 9:8

My beloved, it is my nature to be gracious. I don't change; it is
always my desire to give to my children. I am even gracious to
the wicked. If this was not the case I would judge them immediately and not give them time to repent and believe in me, and so
embrace my will for their lives.

I have shown you my grace by giving you salvation, placing
you in Christ and making you part of my Kingdom. *I am able to*
make all grace abound to you, so that in all things, at all times,
having all that you need, you will abound in every good work. Yes,
this is my word too – *all* things! At *all* times! So you will have *all*
you need.

I always want to extend my grace to you – every day, in every
situation in which you find yourself. There is never a moment of
time when my grace is not available to you. Why do you find this
so difficult to believe, when I have already given you the fullness
of life that is in Christ?

I want to *give* to you. Yes, give, give, give. This means I want
you to receive, receive, receive. What is the point of me giving if
you are not prepared to receive? The value of keeping your relationship with me on the right footing is that it is then far easier
for you to receive what I want to give.

I am your Father and you are my child. Parents provide for
their children, help them, encourage them and build them up. I
am willing to do all these things for you because of my love for
you. Parents don't expect children to provide for them! I am no
ordinary father, either: I am the Almighty One, who is ready to

do for you the things you could never do for yourself. Don't waste either my grace or my power!

If you don't believe I want to be gracious to you in such ways, then you will not expect me to bless you and answer your prayers. You will not pray with the faith and expectation I want you to have.

I am not asking you to be selfish, for I make clear that my motive in giving to you is so that you will abound in every good work. I want to recreate my generosity in you, for you to be gracious because I am gracious.

Consider this: if you have the ability to help someone but they ignore your offer of help or your advice, doesn't that make you feel frustrated? Isn't it a form of rejection? Well, don't treat me like that, for I am always at hand, ready to help and give you the counsel you need. Let me be the Father, the Counsellor, the Helper I want to be to you. Nothing is too much trouble for me. Nothing is too small a matter for me to care about, or too large a matter to be able to take care of.

Above all, allow me to work *for* you. Yes, there is no limit to what I can do for you if you will only let me. You have watched a small child trying to fix a toy. She goes about the task in completely the wrong way, but refuses all offers of help from her parents. She is determined to be independent! Finally, in frustration, she has to admit defeat and meekly comes to her parents, asking them to mend the toy.

You are often like that, beloved. You try to fix problems in your life. You strive to overcome sin and failure. Although I am with you, ready to help, you ignore me. In your pride you are determined to overcome the problem in your own strength. You have been influenced by the world's lie that God only helps those who help themselves.

Beloved, I help those who know they cannot help themselves! Why not admit defeat? Have I not said that in your flesh, in your natural life, there dwells nothing good, that apart from me you can do nothing? So why try to overcome problems with

25

your natural abilities when you have all my spiritual and super-natural resources available to you? Why try to do without me what can only be done by me?

You have to decide: are you going to mend the toy or am I? We can't both do it at the same time! Either you trust in my grace or you trust in yourself. I haven't come into your life on a power-sharing basis; we can't both be in control. A car cannot be driven by two people at once. You have to decide who is going to drive your life. Isn't it time to move over to the passenger seat and allow me to take over the controls? I know the direction in which to take you.

Do you see your confusion? You like the idea of me giving you all you need on every occasion, but you still want to be in control. I am not giving you all the riches of my grace for you to drive in your own direction, but to allow me to take you in the direction I have chosen for you as my disciple.

Romans 11:6   2 Peter 1:3   Galatians 3:26–28

Grace to the Humble

He gives us more grace. That is why Scripture says:
'God opposes the proud but gives grace to the humble.'
James 4:6

My beloved, I give grace to the humble; but I pull down the proud.

Do you remember that Jesus said He had a gentle and humble heart? Yes, He was the man of power and great authority, but at all times He remained submitted to me. He never once went against my authority or my will. He made it clear that He had been sent to do not His own will but my heavenly will.

Independence is a form of pride. My children are guilty of pride when they depend on themselves, when they make decisions independently of me, without being concerned for my will and purpose. I don't give grace to the proud to support them in their independence, for that would be to defeat my own purposes. Instead, I have to discipline them. I will always give them the grace to repent and humble themselves before me. Then I can lift them much higher than they could ever exalt themselves. It is a self-defeating thing to exalt yourself.

Obviously, beloved, I will not give you grace to oppose my will; **but I will always give you grace to do my will**. It is very simple, really!

You easily become frustrated when you act independently and strain against what I want for you. Nothing seems to work out for you, no matter how hard you try! What you are able to accomplish in the flesh is of no consequence to me. As far as I am concerned, the only things that count are those you do in obedience to me, to fulfil my will and purpose. My divine resources are available to enable you to do *my* will, not yours.

I don't dispense my grace in a mechanical way, but within the context of the relationship we enjoy together. I always know what is best for you. There have been times when you have asked me to do certain things for you. If I had granted your request it would have hindered my purpose for you and would have caused you unnecessary difficulties. Even though you didn't appreciate it at the time, later you realized that I had acted in your own best interests.

Events always prove me right! I always know what I am doing, and sometimes I have to over-ride your enthusiasms. I want to keep you humble, submitted to me, not only so that my purposes can be fulfilled, but because this is in your own best interests. Then I can raise you up in my purposes, which are more glorious than your own.

It's a matter of the heart, isn't it, beloved? **I am encouraging you to have a humble heart, like that of Jesus; desiring to do my will, not your own; trusting in me and not in yourself; learning to live by grace and not self-effort. And understanding that there is no end to the blessings of my grace that I will pour into your life day by day to enable these objectives to be realized.**

I know what to give, how to give, and the right time to give. So trust me.

Romans 8:32   Ephesians 1:7   Matthew 11:29

Grace for My Purpose

*Through him, and for his name's sake, we received grace and
apostleship to call people from among all the Gentiles to the
obedience that comes from faith.*
Romans 1:5

My beloved, Jesus made it clear that those who were not with
Him were against Him. I choose those who at one time were
against me, I turn their lives around and make them part of my
Kingdom *now* so that they might live for me *now*. I don't judge
them in the way I could, but extend my grace to them instead.

No one has demonstrated this transformation more obviously
than my servant Paul. As Saul the Pharisee, he thought he was
serving me with great zeal. In fact, he was opposing me by
rejecting Jesus and persecuting those who loved Him. I had to
show him how blind he had been. Religious zeal can blind people
to the truth; they put their faith in their religion rather than in
me. Having realized his foolishness, Saul turned to me with all his
heart and embraced the gospel fully. The one who had persecuted
the Church became the great apostle to the Gentiles.

This was my calling on his life. Who else would think of
choosing one of my greatest opponents to become one of my
chief spokesmen? This demonstrates the transforming power of
the life I offer all who turn to me. I change them from the people
they were into the people I want them to be. They don't become
all I desire them to be overnight; they don't become perfect in
every way immediately. But my Spirit comes to live in them to
transform them into my likeness and enable them to do all I ask
of them, all I have planned for their lives.

From the moment of your new birth, you were made holy.
This means you were called and set apart for me and for my
purposes. Instead of opposing my purposes any longer, Paul

embraced my will for his life and gave himself wholeheartedly to me and then to the ministry to which I had called him. I want you to do likewise! **Give yourself wholeheartedly to me and to the ministry I have for you.**

Some reject salvation. Others who have tasted of my salvation reject my grace subsequently by rejecting the ministry I have for them. They want the benefits of salvation, but still persist in walking in their own ways. They have their own dreams, aspirations and agendas for what they want to do with their lives. As a result, they have little awareness of my grace working with them day by day, for I make my grace available for my purposes, not theirs.

I want you to know my grace working with you day by day, enabling you to do what I have called and chosen you to do. Such a life is both rich and joyful, for there is no greater joy than knowing you have yielded your life fully to me and are fulfilling the purpose I have for you.

What is my ministry for you? First and foremost, to reveal my love to those you live and work with, and to those with whom you worship. To seek first my Kingdom and righteousness; to allow Jesus to express the life of His Kingdom in and through you with the certain knowledge that everything you need will be added to you, as I have promised. You will not have to worry or be anxious.

My Kingdom is righteousness, peace and joy in the Holy Spirit. As you yield to His leadership, He will guide you into all truth. He will show you what to believe in every situation that confronts you. He will give you the right words to speak and tell you what to do. He will always point you to my grace.

Not only do you live in Christ; His Spirit lives in you. Why grieve His presence and power? Why do you think you will be more successful trusting in your own wisdom and abilities than in His? Are you afraid to seek the fulfilment of my plans for your life? Do you think I will be too demanding? Haven't I made it clear enough that I will always be with you and will make all grace abound to you, no matter what direction I lead you in? So why be afraid? I am your Father! I know what potential you have, and lovingly I will nurture you so this can be fully realized.

John 6:38   1 Peter 5:6   Romans 4:17   Ephesians 1:7–8

Abundant Grace

*In him we have redemption through his blood, the forgiveness
of sins, in accordance with the riches of God's grace that he
lavished on us with all wisdom and understanding.*
Ephesians 1:8

My beloved, my servant Paul never lost sight of the magnitude of
the grace I had extended towards him, which is why he spoke of
grace in such lavish terms. He spoke of my glorious grace that is
given to all in Christ, and said that I lavish my grace on all who
believe in Him.

Paul regarded himself as the chief of sinners because he
persecuted the Church and cast his vote against many who
died for their faith in Jesus. Yet even these sins were covered by
the blood. Instead of judging him and condemning him in the
way he deserved, I saved him, cleansed him, anointed him,
used him to establish churches and to bear much fruit for the
glory of my name. This was the measure of my grace towards
him. No wonder he had such a revelation of the lavish nature
of my love!

That same grace is available to all my disciples. I lavish my
grace on those saved from the gutters of life, from lives of abject
depravity. I lavish my grace on those who before turning to me
were full of religious pride and self-righteousness, thinking that
they were good in themselves and regarding others with pride
and disdain.

I lavish my grace on those who feel totally inadequate and
rejected, whose lives seem to have no direction or purpose, who
have considered themselves useless, a laughing-stock even,
because it appears they have no natural giftings or abilities to
commend them. I take hold of their lives and give them direction and purpose. I show them that in Christ their lives have

great value and worth, though outside Him they could see their lives had none.

Beloved, the condition of my children in their former lives is no longer relevant. Once they have been born again and have tasted my grace, everything is different for them. This is why Jesus tells you not to look back. As a new creation, each is able to live according to my grace instead of resisting or opposing it. And the greater their revelation of grace, the more they will love me. Those who are forgiven much, love much. The deeper the pit out of which I have saved them, the more thankful they will be, with no desire to look back.

So, beloved, don't live in the past! It is who you are now that matters, as a child of my grace, living in Christ. You are no longer a victim of your past; now you are a victor, one who in Christ has overcome the past and has a brilliant future ahead.

Nothing in all creation can separate you from my love. Therefore, nothing in all creation can separate you from my grace, beloved, for I express my love for you through my grace.

To abide in the love of Jesus is to live in the grace I have made available through Him. I have chosen to lavish my grace on *you*, not by mistake or in any haphazard way but according to my wisdom and understanding. I know, therefore, the ways in which my grace needs to be extended to you and evidenced in your life day by day as the practical outworking of my love for you. My grace available to you is as great as the grace Saul of Tarsus experienced. That grace transformed his life and will transform yours also. **You are not disqualified from my blessings because of what you were or because of any past traumatic experiences**. Obey Jesus! Don't look back; look to Him to supply all your needs according to the riches of His glory. He leads you forward in the new life, not back into the old.

Romans 8:30   James 4:6   James 4:10

Grace to You

Grace and peace to you from God our Father
and the Lord Jesus Christ.
Philippians 1:2

Beloved, the apostles began their letters by desiring to impart to their readers the blessings of my grace. They often ended their letters in similar fashion: 'Grace and peace to you from God our Father and the Lord Jesus Christ'.

My Spirit is the channel of this grace, but I am the source of all grace. I give to you in the name of my Son through the channel of the Holy Spirit. So the whole Trinity of God is involved in blessing you with grace and peace.

The apostles appreciated that the only way their readers could accomplish anything worthwhile was by my grace working with them, in them and through them. People can read these words at the beginning of the epistles and receive nothing. They can regard them only as a greeting and not receive them as a personal word from me. If, however, you accept these words with faith, you can receive an impartation of my grace through them, in whatever way you need to receive blessing from me at that particular time.

I have revealed various aspects of my nature by the various names by which I am to be known, each one revealing something of the ways in which I want to relate to my children. I will remind you of some of these great names.

I am the Lord, the Almighty One. I am the Lord of heaven and earth. Is anything too hard for me? Of course not! I am the Lord of hosts, of the vast multitudes in heaven and earth who love me. Nothing is impossible for me.

I Am Who I Am, and you live in me. You live in the great I Am, the One who brought all creation into being, the One who existed before everything He made! Am I not able to bring to completion the purposes I have for my creation?

I am the Lord your Righteousness. I regard you as righteous because you live in the Righteous One. He has put you right with me. I will enable you to walk in righteousness, to be in right relationship with me and receive the grace and power to do what I consider right. To trust in yourself will lead inevitably to unrighteousness, for in your flesh, your natural life, there is nothing good.

I am Holy, and I am the Lord who sanctifies you. Draw on my resources of holiness by the Holy Spirit who lives in you. He will enable you to live the holy life, a life pleasing to me that reflects my character and fulfils my will. Stand against every temptation to compromise, to live according to the standard of the world, instead of revealing the life of my Kingdom: righteousness, peace and joy in the Holy Spirit.

I am the Lord your Peace. You are at peace with me when you do my will, and when you trust me even in the midst of conflict and turmoil. Knowing you are in my care and under my protection enables you to experience and enjoy my peace.

I am the Lord who is present with you. So you need never depend on yourself. I am your constant companion and helper. I will never leave you or forsake you. My presence shall go with you and I will give you rest.

I am the Lord your Healer. When Jesus went to the cross, He bore your infirmities and carried your sicknesses; by His stripes you are healed. I can give you grace to bear sickness, but I want you to have faith in me to overcome the disease. I want you to believe not only that I am able to heal you, but that I desire to do so because it is my nature to heal, to restore and make whole those who suffer in spirit, soul or body.

I am the Lord your Provider. My beloved, I will never come to the end of my giving to you. It is my joy as your Father to provide for you. I don't begrudge anything I give by my grace. I give abundantly, with a generous heart, and always in love.

I am the Lord your Banner, your Victory. I am He who fights for you and gives you the grace to overcome whatever comes against you. You will overcome by the blood of the Lamb, Jesus, who was slain for you, and by the word of your testimony. In Him you have total authority and victory over all the power of the evil one.

I am the Lord your Shepherd. I am your Pastor, therefore. I provide for you so that you will not want; I lead you to rich pastures beside still water, and in paths of righteousness for my name's sake. If you wander from my ways, I pursue you to bring you back into my will.

Beloved, when you see the words 'Grace to you ...' pause to think and be thankful for all I give to you as my child: my almighty power; my righteousness and holiness; my peace; and all the comfort and strength that comes from knowing I am with you always. Yes, I give health and provision. I am your victory, and through my grace I enable you to overcome. And I am your Good Shepherd, who leads you and cares for you in every way.

Do you get the point? Concentrate on who I am, not on yourself. Fix your eyes on Jesus, the Author and Perfector of your faith. Your real identity is in Him, not in the weak failure you used to be!

Ephesians 1:6   2 Corinthians 5:17   1 Corinthians 1:28–29

Grace from Beginning to End

This is the true grace of God. Stand fast in it.
1 Peter 5:12

Beloved, everything in the Christian life begins and ends in grace. Some with religious backgrounds have legalistic attitudes. They taste my grace and walk in freedom for a while, only to return to their former religious and legalistic attitudes and traditions. They have become deceived. It is my purpose that they continue to walk in freedom by continuing to live in my grace.

I sent my Son, Jesus, to be crucified in order to deliver my people from the curse of legalistic religious observance. He came to impart life and freedom, not religious formalism.

Why do people find it so much easier to return to religious attitudes? It is easier to live by a form of religion than to live by faith. It is simpler to believe you can please me by religious observance than to walk in a relationship of love with me, receiving the blessings I want to impart through my grace.

Others depart from the way of grace by abusing that grace. They think that, because I am merciful and generous, it doesn't matter how they live; they imagine I will easily overlook their failure and sin. The fact is that they have little or no regard for my righteous and holy will.

Listen, beloved: I call my children to repentance. This involves more than the forgiveness of sins, but a turning away from those sins. Those who abuse my grace soon find they have returned to bondage. Once again they are in the grip of the sins that please them but displease me. The sense of my presence and power in their lives rapidly recedes as a result.

Is there a way back? Yes, the way of repentance, of turning away from sin and once again embracing the life of righteousness. **I don't give any of my children the grace to sin, but the**

grace to be delivered from the power of sin and to live in the righteousness I desire for them.

I hear some of my children boast that they no longer live under law but under grace; yet they abuse my grace. They have cast off the restraints of the law and act as if they have the freedom to do whatever they please. This is an abuse of my grace. I have given grace to enable them to fulfil the law in their lives, not to act as if my will doesn't matter!

Love for me is expressed through obedience, through the grace I give to obey. When Jesus came, full of grace and truth, He lived in obedience to me; He didn't cast off all restraint and do as He pleased.

I don't want any of my children to be bound by either sin or legalistic religion; I want them to live in the freedom of the life and love Jesus came to give them. Then my joy will be in them and their joy will be full. Sin and legalistic religion are the easy options that the flesh favours. Faith and loving obedience are the way of my Spirit.

It is not my will for any child of mine to be careless in the way they live, so that sin is able to gain the upper hand. It is true that where sin abounds, grace all the more abounds. But this is not an excuse for wilful disobedience. It simply points to the truth that no sin is beyond my grace. I am always ready to restore those who turn back to me.

The grace I make available to my children is the grace to obey, not disobey!

1 Corinthians 15:10   Jeremiah 23:6b   Colossians 1:6

17

Mutual Love

I love you, O L<small>ORD</small>, my strength.
Psalm 18:1

We love because he first loved us.
1 John 4:19

My beloved, I have declared my love for you, not only in words, but in what I have done for you. I have forgiven you, given you my life and have placed my Spirit within you. Such love demands a response of love! Is this what you are afraid of, that my love for you is so great that I require a love from you that would be impossible for you to give? I can understand such fears, but they are groundless. Let me explain.

In a loving relationship love has to be mutual. Because I love you I want you to love me with all your heart, mind, soul and strength. My love for you is wholehearted, and I want your love for me to be wholehearted too.

As I express my love for you in what I have done for you, so I want your love for me to be expressed in positive action, not just in words.

I am aware you are only able to love because I have first loved you; your love for me can only be a response to the love I have for you. So the more you understand my love for you, the more you will love me. You certainly won't grow in love for me by looking at yourself, thinking your love is inadequate!

My love for you is unconditional. I loved you *before* you loved me. Before I created the world I knew you would become my child and have a significant part to play in my purposes; otherwise I would not have chosen you. I know this is difficult for you to understand; nevertheless it is true. If I chose you before the creation of the world, that decision could not depend on anything you had done. Because I predestined you in love to be my child, my love for you could not be determined by your performance or actions. **I love you because I love you!** And I want you to enjoy a loving relationship with me.

I am always there for you, ready to strengthen you and help you. You cannot fulfil my purpose in your own strength; so I don't leave you to your own devices. I am with you always and will never leave you. You see, my beloved, I am faithful in the way I love. My love is sure, certain and steadfast; it doesn't change with mood or circumstances. And I don't stop loving you because of the inadequacy of your love for me.

Jesus prayed that my love would be in you; and this is exactly what you have received through the power of my Holy Spirit. **Yes, my beloved, you have my love in you; the same love I had for Jesus I have for you, and the same love that was in Him I have placed in you.**

This is the love that enabled Him to obey me. That love will also inspire obedience in you. For those who truly love me obey my commands. They want to live as the disciples, as friends of Jesus.

Although you have my love in you, you don't always choose to obey, do you, beloved? Sometimes you choose to love yourself instead of me, by being selfish, by closing your ears to my word and stubbornly refusing to do what I tell you.

Such behaviour strains our relationship, doesn't it? When you place your concentration on self you lose your sense of my love for you. At such times you begin to question and doubt my love, and become aware of your own inadequacy and lack instead. That way of thinking causes you to feel insecure. Then it is even more difficult to believe my love for you. 'How can God love a failure?' you reason.

My beloved, you are not a failure: you are my child, precious and honoured in my sight. You only feel a failure because you focus on yourself. Don't you see? You put your trust in the one you look at! If you trust in yourself, no matter how able you are, you will feel inadequate, you will question my love for you, and you will inevitably fail.

It is wiser to keep your eyes on me and my love for you! Then you will realize that I am the strength of your life. All my resources are available to you to help and enable you, no matter what challenges you have to face. By trusting in my love, you will always be able to overcome. Trusting in yourself will lead to inevitable failure.

Because I am with you always, you can talk to me at any time. I always listen and am ready to give you the grace to do whatever you have to do. So, my beloved, be wise. Keep your focus on my love and you will be able to trust me to give you the strength to serve me, to love others and do whatever you have to do to fulfil my plan and destiny for you.

Galatians 3:13   Ephesians 1:5   John 17:26

You Live in the Positive Kingdom

No one knows the Father except the Son and those
to whom the Son chooses to reveal him.
Matthew 11:27

My beloved, does it seem that your old life still has a large influence on your life? This is only because you don't believe fully in what I have done for you.

Nothing in your past can help you to live by faith in me now. Believe what I tell you. The old has gone; it is dead, buried and finished with. Like Paul, you have been crucified with Christ. It is no longer the old you that lives; your new identity is Christ in you. The life you are to live now, in your body, you are to live by faith in the Son of God, who loved you and gave His life for you.

Instead of doubting these truths about yourself, thank me for them. Be thankful that Jesus has chosen to reveal me to you, that He has made it possible for you to be loved, appreciated and accepted by the God of heaven and earth, your Father! Now you can live the new life without being in bondage to sin and failure.

Don't think of yourself as the person you used to be, but as the one I see you to be now: alive in Christ. He is your Life. He is your righteousness. He is your Peace. He is your Healer and Provider. He is your Shepherd so that you shall not want. **You are alive in Him.**

Why do I have to keep reminding you of these truths? Because it is so easy for you to slip back to the old way of thinking, where you saw yourself as the centre of your life, when you thought that your acceptance as a person depended on what you did, rather than on what Christ did for you. There were so many negatives in your thinking then, weren't there? In Christ there are no negatives; everything about Him is positive.

It is simple to see whether you are walking in the truth of my love by applying this simple test: are you living in the negative or the positive?

Everything about the devil and the dominion of darkness is negative. He is the father of all lies, the deceiver, the accuser, the thief who steals, kills and destroys. He wants to cause condemnation, failure and fear, and to place people in bondage to sickness, oppression and everything that would curse them. He tempts people to sin and deny the truth.

By contrast, everything about Jesus and His Kingdom is positive. He is the Lord and Saviour, the Way, the Truth and the Life. He is the Good Shepherd who lays down His life for the sheep. He is full of compassion, mercy and grace. He is with you always to love and bless you. He is the Light.

What a contrast between darkness and light, between the negative and the positive kingdoms!

You used to belong to the negative kingdom; when you were born again you were transferred into the positive Kingdom of the Son I love. Leave all those negatives behind, therefore, and live a positive life.

You can tell when you are being negative or positive, can't you, beloved? You no longer belong to the negative; my life within you is full of love, joy, peace, power and everything that is positive. When you are walking in the revelation of my love for you, you are filled with the positive. When you become negative you have slipped away from the revelation of my truth.

You are a child of the light. So walk in the light of my word and believe what I say, not what the liar says about you! He wants you to believe you are still in bondage to your past, that you are not truly made new and so cannot lay hold of your rich inheritance. He encourages everything that is negative. The devil wants you to judge and condemn others, to be dissatisfied, to grumble and complain about your circumstances. He encourages gossip and back-biting. He wants you to feel depressed, discouraged and defeated.

Remember, the devil is jealous of you because he was thrown

out of heaven, where you belong. He has no rich inheritance as you have. If he is under the feet of Christ, he is under your feet also, for you live in Christ. Feed on the Living Bread that came down from heaven, not on the devil's lies. You are who I say you are. You have what I say you have – authority over all the power of the evil one. You are able to abide in my love, not his negative lies. This is why Jesus tells you to throw off the negative but to put on the positive, to put on Christ.

Don't allow the devil to gloat over you! I am ready to forgive all those negatives you have allowed, so he will have no ground to stand on.

You don't expect to find any negatives in heaven, do you? Remember, you are to pray that my Kingdom will come, that my will shall be done on earth as in heaven. It is my will, therefore, to see all those negatives disappear from your life and for you to express my love and grace, which are always positive.

Matthew 5:14   Romans 8:29   1 John 4:19

19

I Am Faithful to My Word

God, who has called you into fellowship with his Son,
Jesus Christ our Lord, is faithful.
1 Corinthians 1:9

My beloved, sometimes you have depended on others and they have failed you. There have been disappointments, times of rejection and even occasions when you have felt betrayed.

I am faithful; I have never failed you. You can trust me knowing that I will never reject you. You can depend on my words of truth; they will never change. Heaven and earth will pass away but my words will never pass away! They are not open to debate. They are the words of life that are able to set you free and enable you to live in freedom.

You can depend on my word as you would depend on me. Submitting to my authority involves submission to the authority of my word: the eternal, unchanging truth of your God. Holding fast to my word will keep you from the lies and deception of the enemy, from the ideas and opinions of others and from all that is false.

Without faith in the authority of my word, you will live swayed by your own opinions. You will make decisions and reach conclusions based on your own human reason rather than divine revelation. Your faith will be in your own understanding and you will easily be deceived by the enemy. He is the deceiver of the brethren. His aim, therefore, is to encourage you to believe anything other than my word. For that which is not the truth must be deception. So he wants you to have opinions of your own that conflict with what I say and the revelation of truth I give you in scripture.

My thoughts are higher than your thoughts and my ways greater than your ways. Depending on your own reason and understanding will always result in limiting my power in your life. And that is precisely what the devil wants. Faith in my word stretches you beyond the limitations of human reason and opinions.

Beloved, you cannot separate me from my words. I am Truth, so my words are words of truth. I am Life, for my words are the words of life. I am Almighty; these are the words of power. You have been called into fellowship with Jesus Christ, the Word of God!

Do you understand the implications of what I say? You can hear my voice simply by reading the words of scripture. Put those words into practice and you will not only obey my will; you will stand on the sure rock of truth so that you will never be shaken.

This is why I want you to be a person of the word. Yes, these words are spirit and life for you – healing to your whole body, even! They are the Rock on which your life is to be built.

John 6:63   1 John 1:3   John 8:31–32

20

Faith Is Agreement with Me

And without faith it is impossible to please God.
Hebrews 11:6

Beloved, I have called you to be a disciple of Jesus. To follow Jesus you have to live in agreement with Him: you cannot walk with Him if you disagree with Him. And so, beloved, faith is living in agreement with His words, for He cannot be separated from what He says. How can you walk together unless you agree together? It is not for Jesus to agree with you, but you with Jesus! To agree with Him is to agree with me. To walk with Him is to walk with me.

There are many things you don't yet understand. I don't wait until your understanding is perfect before I walk with you or allow you to walk with me. No, as we walk together much revelation takes place, so that your understanding is increased and your faith enlarged.

It is when you disagree with me that the problems begin; when you think that you know better than I do, or that your knowledge and understanding exceeds the revelation of my word. Your opinions will die with you; my words live for ever! Heaven and earth will pass away, but my words will not pass away; they are the words of eternal life.

Your faith cannot be in me if you disagree with what I say. It is for you to agree with me, not me with you!

Sometimes I wait until you see things as I do before I intervene with power to change a situation. While you stubbornly hold on to your opinions you frustrate my desire to help you; and you feel frustrated yourself because it seems then that I don't want to help.

On the other hand, the agreement of faith is very powerful. This is why Jesus told people their faith had healed them. They not only agreed with Jesus that He *could* heal them, but knew that He *would* do so. 'Do you believe I am able to do this?' Jesus asked. The simple answer of agreement: 'Yes, Lord,' brought the response, 'Go on your way: your faith has healed you.'

Beloved, you can see what power is unleashed by agreeing with me, for then you can exercise the authority I give you to pray and minister to others in my name. Submission to me releases my authority into your life.

You cannot truly pray in my name, on my behalf, unless what you pray agrees with my word. Neither can you do anything in my name, unless it is what I tell you. When you obey my word you act in agreement with me, and then you see my grace released supernaturally into your circumstances. It seems that I have taken hold of the situation on your behalf. After all, when you agree with me you agree with God, the Creator, the Almighty, for whom nothing is impossible.

2 Thessalonians 3:3   Luke 21:33   Isaiah 55:8

21

Agree with My Word

I tell you the truth, anyone who has faith in me will
do what I have been doing. He will do even greater
things then these, because I am going to the Father.
John 14:12

My beloved, Jesus is the truth. Every time you agree with what He says you agree with the truth. Whenever you disagree with what He says, this means you must believe something other than the truth; you believe a lie.

The enemy is the father of lies. He has always been a liar and opposes the truth. He opposed Jesus and he still opposes the truth today. He opposes you because you believe the truth. However, the truth is far more powerful than his lies!

Jesus has said that if you continue to trust in His words, you will live as His disciple; you will know the truth and the truth will set you free. In contrast, believing the lies of the enemy, or anything in your own thinking that opposes the truth, will lead to bondage. You see, you place your life under what you believe. If you believe anything that opposes the truth, you place your life under what is false. And you don't want to do that!

When Jesus said things He knew people would find difficult to believe, He prefaced His statement with this phrase: 'I tell you the truth …' Everything Jesus said was the truth; yet some things were so radical people found it almost impossible to accept they could be true. So to pre-empt their unbelief, He emphasized that what He was about to say really was true. He knew they still thought within the limitations of what they could do naturally, instead of seeing what was possible supernaturally through faith in Him.

It seems radical, almost beyond belief, that you can do the same things as Jesus. Nevertheless, this is true. So agree with what Jesus says about *anyone* who has faith, including you!

Unbelief is often encouraged by experience. It is difficult to believe you can do the same things as Jesus if you have never done such things. Don't you see that until you agree with what He says, you cannot see Him working in your life in this way? If you are in agreement with Him, you will do the same works as He did. It is as simple as that!

So first you need to come into the agreement of faith with what Jesus has said about you as a believer. It is not as if you had chosen to believe you could do the same things as Him because you had grandiose ideas about yourself. No, it was Jesus who said this about you.

What did Jesus do? He manifested all the qualities or characteristics of the Holy Spirit. All these qualities can be reproduced in you because you are filled with the same Spirit – His Spirit.

Jesus healed the sick, raised the dead, cast out demons; and He sent His disciples to do these same things. These are signs or evidences of the presence of the Kingdom of God among those who believe when the gospel is preached; for my Kingdom is not a matter of talk, but of power. These same signs and wonders follow believers today when they share the good news with others and exercise the authority of my Kingdom.

Does this stretch your faith? Is this beyond what you imagine could happen in your own experience? Well, remember, **I am able to do far more than all you can ask or imagine, according to my power that is at work within you**. Jesus said that you would receive power when you received the Holy Spirit, the supernatural power of God that is far greater than the natural and can transform situations. That power is in you and can work through you, beloved.

However, it is one thing to receive the Holy Spirit, another to see the rivers of life flowing out of you because you believe! Yes, it requires the agreement of faith to see the power within you released. Then not only will you see signs and wonders being done through the agreement of faith that enables you to act in the name of Jesus, but you will also use all the gifts of the Holy

Spirit that are available to you. Yes, whatever gift you need at any given moment is available to you.

Listen, beloved: I want you to do the same things as Jesus. This is not some unrealistic, spiritual theory; it is my will for you. You can exercise the faith, authority and power that will make this possible.

John 14:12   Matthew 10:1   Mark 16:15–18

22

You Are 'At One' with Me

God presented him as a sacrifice of atonement,
through faith in his blood.
Romans 3:25

My beloved, I sent Jesus to atone for your sins and the sins of the whole world. Do you realize the implications of this? Through His sacrifice on the cross, He satisfied my wrath and judgment on sin. He bore the punishment for sin you deserve, He took all your sin, guilt and shame upon Himself. He justified you, made you totally acceptable in my sight.

He did even more. 'To atone for you' means He restored you to the place of being 'at one' with me. Yes, my beloved, through the sacrifice of His blood on the cross you are now at one with me, now and for all eternity.

While on earth, Jesus lived at one with me. This is why His death could be a valid sacrifice offered on behalf of all who are not at one with me. No lesser sacrifice could have achieved my objective of bringing you back into unity with me and enabling you to live at one with me.

Not only did Jesus accomplish this for you on the cross, He also demonstrated by His life how to live at one with me. You are able to live in agreement with me. To live at one with me in Christ is to agree with what He reveals about me, about my love and grace. It is to agree that you live in Him and He in you. It is to agree that because you are in Him you have the same resources available to you that He had. What is true of Him is true of you, because you are at one with Him. Therefore I can impart to you the same life and blessings I imparted to Him. It was this truth that Jesus was concerned to impress on His disciples, amazing though it seems.

You don't have to guess or try to imagine what it means to be at one with Him and therefore with me; Jesus Himself made this abundantly clear. So I want you to listen to what He teaches, for in Him you are able to relate to me as He did.

You see, beloved, you have both a soul and a spirit. When you were born again my Spirit came to live in your spirit. The Spirit of Christ lives in you now and He is in perfect agreement with me. The same Spirit who lived in Jesus and enabled Him to do all that He did lives in you to enable you to do the same things. This is the same Spirit by whom He was raised from the dead. This shows you the power that is in your spirit! I did not give you a spirit of fear, but of power, love and a sound mind.

You have living in you the One who enables you to live in agreement with me. However, your soul – your natural self-life – is not yet in such unity with me. That is why you experience so much conflict within yourself. Your soul consists of your mind, emotions and will. This means that you have two minds, two sets of emotions and two distinct wills within you.

You have your natural mind in your soul and the mind of Christ in your spirit. These two minds think on entirely different levels: one naturally, the other supernaturally. If you are double-minded you are unstable in all your ways and cannot expect to receive anything from me. So my desire is for you to have singleness of mind, so you can avail yourself of my grace.

The only way to have singleness of mind is to submit your natural mind (the way you think, your ideas and opinions) to the mind of Christ, the mind of my Spirit within your spirit. Then you will be in agreement with me and my power will be released in and through you.

You have within you your natural feelings and emotions which form part of your soul life; but you also have the witness or feelings of my Spirit within your spirit. As my disciple, you learn that to follow your own feelings often causes disaster, whereas to follow the witness of the Spirit guides you into the truth.

You have your own natural will that is another aspect of your soul life, and you have my will within you, Christ in you. Even Jesus had His natural will, but also my will within Him because my Spirit lived in Him. This is why He prayed: 'Not my will but yours be done.' He submitted His human will to my divine will; and this is what you are to do also.

My word is like a double-edged sword that divides soul and spirit. It shows you what is of your own natural thinking, feelings and will, and what is of the mind of Christ, the witness of my Spirit and my will for you. To live in agreement with me will therefore often involve denying your way of thinking and submitting to the mind of Christ instead. You will need to obey the witness of my Spirit rather than being led by your own feelings and desires. And, like Jesus, you will need to submit your will to mine.

When you think as I think, denying any negative feelings that contradict my word, and when you submit your will to mine, your soul life is in submission to my Spirit living in your spirit. My life can then flow through your spirit and flood your soul.

My life will even give life to your mortal body and will flow out of you as rivers of living water.

This is what I want to see: that my life not only pours into you, but that it flows out of you to the benefit of others!

Hebrews 2:17   Romans 12:1–2   John 7:37–9

23

At One with Jesus

For the word of God is living and active. Sharper than
any double-edged sword, it penetrates even to dividing
soul and spirit, joints and marrow; it judges the thoughts
and attitudes of the heart.
Hebrews 4:12

I want to impress on you, beloved, that through the atonement
you are already at one with me in the Spirit. The applications of
this truth are immense, for you share in all the benefits and
blessings that were given to Jesus because you are at one with
Him. Here are some of these wonderful truths. Remember, they
are already truths about you spiritually. As you learn to live as
my disciple, submitting your soul life to the Spirit, these truths
will be expressed increasingly in your experience.

Don't push any of these revelations to one side, thinking they
could not possibly be true for you. These blessings are already
yours, and as you learn to live at one with me, you will do
exactly what my word says you can do.

When your soul and body act independently of your spirit,
you act in the flesh, not in my Spirit. Remember the flesh and the
Spirit are in direct opposition; they will never agree.

Because you are at one with Jesus, you belong to me. He
has paid the price for you. Your flesh will want to deny this, to be
independent and encourage you to think that your life is still
your own.

**Because you are at one with Jesus, you are at one with
the Word of God**. Agreeing with what He says will release His
life and power into your life. You cannot live at one with Him
and disagree with what He said! However, your flesh will
always disagree with the truth, which is why every day it has to
be denied.

Because you are at one with Jesus, you are at one with the One who is the Light. You have become a child of light and can walk in the light of the truth, standing against the darkness of all that is negative and in opposition to the revelation of my word.

Because you are at one with Jesus you are able to receive one blessing after another from the fullness of His grace. Your flesh encourages you to live in your own strength, but trying to solve everything in your own natural abilities is utterly opposed to my grace.

Because you are at one with Jesus, I place all my resources in your hands. You can draw upon them by faith, just as He did. Or you can walk in the flesh, depending on yourself.

Because you are at one with Jesus, I call you to share in His work, which is to believe in Him, the One I sent to be your Lord and Saviour. Without faith it is impossible to please me, and all my purposes are accomplished through faith.

Because you are at one with Jesus, your 'food' is the same as His 'food': to do my will and to finish the work I give you to do. The flesh will encourage you to fulfil your own plans and, even if you embark on pleasing me, to give up before my purpose for you is completed.

Because you are at one with Jesus, I will work through you. I worked through Jesus and I will work through you. The flesh is proud and says, 'I will do it myself.'

Because you are at one with Jesus, you are able to live as a child of your heavenly Father, with all the inheritance and authority this implies. Your flesh tells you that you cannot expect to receive anything from me because you are such a useless failure!

Because you are at one with Jesus, you can do nothing by yourself. He was not able to do anything apart from me, and you are not able to do anything apart from Him.

Because you are at one with Jesus, I will reveal my love to you and will show you what I am doing. The flesh doesn't like prayer and so opposes the idea of spending time waiting on me, listening to the voice of my Spirit and becoming sensitive to what I am doing.

Beloved, don't deny your unity with Jesus because these truths seem too great to accept. The more you appreciate that the purpose of the cross was to make you one with me, the more you will be able to live in the good of the life Jesus came to give you. So rejoice in these truths, and in the others that are to follow. Concentrate on the Spirit, and you will not gratify the desires of the flesh.

John 6:29   John 4:34   Galatians 3:26

24

Blessings from Being At One with Jesus

And our fellowship is with the Father
and with his Son, Jesus Christ.
1 John 1:3

My beloved, because you are at one with Jesus you are at one with me. **You are at one with God: Father, Son and Holy Spirit**. Isn't this amazing?

This is what I created humanity for: to live in fellowship, in unity, with me, sharing my life and my love. Sin destroyed that unity with me, but now through the cross that fellowship has been restored. And there are many more blessings that result from being at one with Jesus!

Because you are at one with Jesus, I have placed my seal of approval on you, my promised Holy Spirit. I myself will feed you with the Living Bread that came down from heaven and I will use you to impart my life to the world. Your flesh encourages you to look at self; my Spirit directs you to my words of truth and encourages you to believe what I say.

Because you are at one with Jesus I will never drive you away. I will draw you closer and closer to me. Your flesh thinks it is impossible for you to be near me or to know me intimately.

Because you are at one with Jesus, you are at one with the One who gave His life for the world. So you, too, are to make your body a living sacrifice, holy and acceptable in my sight. Your flesh encourages you to look after yourself; it is essentially selfish and self-centred.

Because you are at one with Jesus, you can even perform miraculous deeds in His name. It will be seen plainly that the things you do are done through God. Your self-life says such things would be impossible for you, that I would never do anything great for you or through you.

Because you are at one with Jesus, you are able to speak the words I give you to speak. The flesh is full of opinions and ideas which certainly do not come from me! Most of them contradict my word and my way of working.

Because you are at one with Jesus, you need judge no one yourself, but are to leave all judgment to Him. You will only judge as you hear from Him. The flesh is full of judging, critical and condemning attitudes.

Because you are at one with Jesus, you have His life in you. I will bear witness that it is I who called you to speak and act in His name. The flesh encourages you to live at the natural level, not in the supernatural power of my Spirit. When you are more conscious of self than of me, you can even forget that I am around!

Because you are at one with Jesus, you will fulfil my will, the plan and destiny I have for your life. The flesh has no vision; you simply exist and your life has no true significance.

Because you are at one with Jesus, you will seek to give me honour in all things. You will live as a child of truth and there will be nothing false about you. The flesh is sensitive and totally unreliable; it wants to honour self and to be recognized rather than honour me.

Because you are at one with Jesus, you are to do nothing on your own, in independence, for that would be a denial of your unity with Him. Your flesh encourages independence.

Because you are at one with Jesus, you will teach others exactly what I give you to teach; my Spirit will command you what to say and how to say it. Your flesh will not listen to what my Spirit says, which is why it is so important to keep your soul submitted to your spirit.

Because you are at one with Jesus, you will always seek to do what pleases me. This involves denying yourself, taking up your cross daily and following in the way I lead you.

Because you are at one with Jesus, you will love me by obeying my commands; you will keep my word and will

never see death. Your flesh-life hates the very idea of obedience and submission.

Because you are at one with Jesus, you will be like Him. You will know me and keep my Word. You will do exactly what I command. Be determined, therefore, that you will not allow your soul to rebel against the revelation of my word.

Can you not see, beloved, that all these things will be evidenced in your life simply through living in unity with Jesus? You don't have to work your way into such a position; I have placed you there. I have made you to be at one with Him. All things are possible for you *now*, as you submit your soul to my Spirit in your spirit.

This is something you need to do at the beginning of every day. Submit yourself to me for the day ahead of you. Tell the Holy Spirit that you submit yourself to Him, spirit, soul and body: to be led by Him; to honour His presence within you; to be sensitive to His voice and obedient to His prompting.

Be thankful that you are at one with Christ, with me, your Father, and with the Holy Spirit who lives in you. Resist anything that would seek to destroy this fellowship, the unity I want us to enjoy.

Ephesians 1:13–14   John 15:9–10   John 6:53–56

25

The Blessings that Result

Your guilt is taken away and your sin atoned for.
Isaiah 6:7

My beloved, there are more mighty truths that flow from the fact that you are at one with Jesus. Receive each revelation with faith. Remember, unbelief is making the wrong choice, choosing to believe something other than the truth.

Because you are at one with Jesus, you can feed my sheep, encouraging them with the truth and loving them as I have loved you. The flesh wants to live for self; the Spirit wants you to live for others.

Because you are at one with Jesus, you will lay down your life for me by laying down your life for others, loving them with the same love with which I love you. To lay down your life is to live for others, a thought abhorrent to the flesh.

Because you are at one with Jesus, I myself am in you and you in me so that you can glorify my name. You will glorify me and I will glorify you in my presence. You can see why Jesus says that you can only be His disciple if you hate your self-life or flesh-life, for in your flesh there dwells nothing good. Your flesh wants to glorify self, not worship and praise me.

Because you are at one with Jesus, He and I make our home with you, and will always be with you in the Spirit, not the flesh.

Because you are at one with Jesus, all my power is available to you through the Holy Spirit. The more fully you are submitted to my authority, the more readily that power can flow through you.

Because you are at one with Jesus, I will show you by my Spirit what must take place in the days to come.

Because you are at one with Jesus, you will live as His friend by doing what He wants you to do. Your self wants

Jesus to be your friend, but does not want to live in obedience as His friend!

Because you are at one with Jesus, I will give you whatever you ask in His name. The Spirit says, 'Believe!'; the flesh says, 'God never answers my prayers.'

Because you are at one with Jesus, the Author and Perfector of your faith, you too will live through faith; you will believe the words I speak to you by my Spirit. The flesh says you should be reasonable: you live in the real world, and to think supernaturally is unreal.

Because you are at one with Jesus, you can exercise His authority. His Spirit in you is greater than he who is in the world. The flesh cannot resist the enemy, because you only walk in the flesh when in some way you are allowing his thinking to influence you.

Because you are at one with Jesus, you have eternal life and He will raise you up. The enemy wants to deceive people into thinking that everything will be fine in the end, no matter what they believe or how they live. He is in direct opposition to the truth.

Because you are at one with Jesus, everything you have comes from Him. That is the fruit of submission. Better you receive the positive life from Jesus than the negatives that come from the world, the flesh and the devil.

Because you are at one with Jesus, you will believe the words I speak to you by my Spirit. I want you to be a listening person, a disciple who knows and responds to the voice of my Spirit.

Because you are at one with Jesus, all He has is yours, and all you have is His. No wonder the devil wants you to walk in the flesh, and so deprive yourself of living in the good of your inheritance!

Because you are at one with Jesus, you will be protected by the power of His name. Walking in the flesh exposes you to the enemy's influence and causes you to be vulnerable.

Because you are at one with Jesus, you have the full measure of His joy within you. The joys the flesh gives you are short-lived and are often followed by remorse. The joys of being at one with Jesus are eternal.

Because you are at one with Jesus, the world will hate you as it hated Him. But be encouraged – He has overcome the world! So you are at one with the One who has overcome the world, the flesh and the devil.

Because you are at one with Jesus, you are in unity with all others who are at one with Him. Don't allow the enemy to cause discord and division.

Because you are at one with Jesus, I will continue to make myself known to you and my love will be in you.

Because you are at one with Jesus, you will show my love to the world as you walk in the Spirit, seeking to please me with harmony between your soul and spirit.

So, beloved, I had good reason in sending Jesus to die for you, to atone for you with His blood. Without that sacrifice, none of this would be possible. Like Him, you can enjoy the life of my Kingdom here on earth and look forward to eternity in heaven. Like Him, you will come to the decision that it doesn't matter much what it costs to be faithful and obedient to me. It is sheer joy to know you please me and fulfil my purpose for you, and that you are a blessing to others, loving, serving and giving to them in my name.

How much of all this is really possible? All of it! Does experience seem so far short of what has been made possible? Sadly, that is often the case. But don't be discouraged, beloved. As you learn to abide in Jesus, to live in the good of your unity with Him, these truths will increasingly be expressed in your life. This is the process which I, as your Father, am overseeing. The more you believe these revelations of truth, the more I like it!

John 15:12–14   John 14:23   John 16:23–24

26

Everything I Have Is Yours

My son ... you are always with me and
everything I have is yours.
Luke 15:31

You are all sons of God by faith in Christ Jesus.
Galatians 3:26

You can see, my beloved, that the greatest problem I have with my children is getting them to believe they have what I say they have, and can do what I have made it possible for them to do.

Everything I have is yours, because you are my child and a co-heir with Jesus. You find it difficult to think of Him as your Brother? I can understand that. He became your Brother by coming to share in your humanity, giving His life for you and making it possible for you to share His risen life.

Everything I have belongs to the Son. Everything that belongs to the Son is made known to you by the Spirit. You have been given the Holy Spirit so that everything belonging to the Father and the Son becomes yours!

Notice, my beloved child, that I am saying all has become yours already. I am not giving you a future promise, but I am speaking of a present reality. **All I have is yours *now*.** What purpose does it serve to have such a rich inheritance if you don't avail yourself of what I have made available to you?

In the parable of the two sons, the father told the prodigal's brother: 'You are always with me and everything I have is yours.' You remember that he was angry that his younger brother had been restored and jealous that, after the prodigal had wasted his inheritance, the father was prepared to lavish further gifts upon him. The older brother was upset because he thought of himself as faithful, yet possessing nothing.

It is good to work diligently; but you cannot work for what can only be given by grace. And so, beloved one, this older brother didn't understand the basic principle of faith: **ask**!

You see, you only ask *with faith* if you are taking hold of what you believe will surely be given you because it is your inheritance. You haven't chosen your own inheritance. I have chosen it for you: every spiritual blessing in Christ. You are like that son in the parable. I can say to you, as my beloved child: **'You are always with me and everything I have is *yours*!'**

I have chosen to give you all things in Christ. There is nothing you can do to change your inheritance, no matter how unworthy you consider yourself. You cannot alter what I have already done. And this is the inheritance I have given you. All that I have is yours. Believe this, and then you can avail yourself of the blessings!

It saddens me to see that many of my beloved ones don't believe what I tell them in my word. They believe their doubts instead of my truth! They listen to the voices that destroy their faith and expectations of blessing, to the voices of unbelief that point out their unworthiness and suggest I wouldn't do anything mighty or miraculous for them. They listen to those who don't walk in agreement with me, instead of listening to the voices of those who believe my word and have seen my power at work as a result.

Beloved, you ignore the truth whenever you look at your negative feelings, imagining that I am far away and don't care about the things that concern you. The older son in the parable made just that same mistake. He was so full of self-righteousness and negativity that he failed to see either the implications of being with me always or the reality of the inheritance that was available to him.

Beloved child, I don't want you to be like that. **I am your Father, you are always with me and everything I have is yours. Believe this**.

You see, the younger son in the parable did believe it, and asked for his inheritance. Because he asked, the father gave it to him. Sadly, he misused it, and that is another important lesson to learn. Don't misuse the gifts I give you! That is a waste; but it is just as much a waste not to lay hold of your inheritance at all. Have you read that verse of scripture that says you do not receive because you do not ask?

I want you to take hold by faith of all that is yours in Christ and to use your inheritance as I intend, for my glory!

Beloved, I have not allotted you a tiny portion. You only think that because that is the level of your faith. Believe what I reveal in my word, that **in Christ all things are yours**. Then you will become bolder in your faith.

You see, you are my child by faith in Christ Jesus, and all children share the right of inheritance. Those who become my children by faith are to live as my children by faith. Faith in my grace enables you to ask and believe that you receive because of my great love for you – not because of the hard work you have done. The younger son had done nothing to deserve his inheritance. An inheritance is given, not earned.

So, my beloved, you are my child by faith. Live as my child by faith and take hold of the rich inheritance that is yours in Christ. For, truly, I am your Father: you are always with me and everything I have is yours!

This only seems unreal to you when you don't believe what I say. **When you do believe you have no problem in approaching me with confidence, knowing that I will indeed give you whatever you ask in the name of Jesus**.

1 Corinthians 1:5   1 Timothy 6:17   2 Corinthians 9:11

27

My Lavish Love

How great is the love the Father has lavished on us,
that we should be called children of God!
1 John 3:1

My beloved, are you beginning to understand how great my love for you is? It is not a begrudging love, but a love that is lavished on you!

Are you beginning to understand my grace? I don't treat you as you deserve. I have chosen to accept you, to place you in Christ and His Spirit in you, to make you a co-heir with Him of all my heavenly riches. **In grace I have chosen to give you everything, although you deserve nothing**.

It's easy to qualify for grace, isn't it? All you have to do is to deserve nothing! However, it is your faith in my grace that enables you to appropriate your inheritance in Christ. Your faith gives you access to my grace every day. This is why Jesus says that your work is to believe in the One I sent; all you accomplish for my glory will be the fruit of what I have given you.

You express faith when you pray. However, be sure your faith is not in your prayer, but in the One to whom you pray! I want you to believe that it is always my desire to give to you. This is why Jesus said, 'Ask and it will be given you,' and 'Everyone who asks receives.' He didn't say it would be given sometimes, if you have been good enough. Neither did He suggest that everyone except you would receive.

My favour is available to *all* my children. I don't prefer you to others, and I don't prefer others to you. All the gifts of my grace are yours, waiting for you to appropriate them by faith. You don't need to be jealous of what others receive!

Sometimes you have felt a sense of injustice, haven't you? You have judged others because you have seen things wrong in their lives, things which seem to indicate they are unworthy to receive blessing from me. You have even thought of yourself as better than them on occasions, that you should be blessed above them!

I never act unjustly. You forget that I give according to my grace, not your worthiness. No one deserves to receive anything from me. In my grace I give according to the faith that my children put in my love and grace. It is possible, therefore, to see things that are not Christ-like in a person for whom I do great things, perhaps by healing them in a wonderful way or by performing a miracle of provision. I won't wait until you are perfectly like my Son before I answer you! And I don't wait until others are perfect before I bless them!

I am ready to forgive you for your jealousy and the way you have judged others. Why not put your trust in my grace, instead of being critical of others or doubting my desire to give to you? Ask and receive! I lavish my love and grace upon you because you are my beloved child.

Luke 11:9   Matthew 21:21–22   Ephesians 1:8

28

I Am Your Shepherd

My sheep listen to my voice; I know them, and they follow me.
John 10:27

My beloved, will you let me pastor you? I am the Good Shepherd, *your* Shepherd. I will care for you so that you lack nothing. It is for the Shepherd to look after the sheep, not for the sheep to look after the Shepherd!

I know each of my sheep by name. I call them, they know my voice and follow me. And look at the way I pastor them!

- **I call them by name**.
- **They know me and I will not allow any to snatch them from me**.
- **They shall not want**.
- **I will lead them to rich pastures**.
- **I will lead them beside still waters of peace**.
- **I will lead them in the way of righteousness so they walk in my ways**.
- **They need fear no evil because I am with them**.
- **Because they follow me, goodness and love will follow them**.
- **I will keep them under my protection. Of course, when they wander off on their own they make themselves vulnerable to attack; but I will follow after them to rescue them from their foolishness**.
- **I meet every need, no matter what their enemies may try to do to them**.
- **I always lead them in triumph in Christ**.

Every one of these benefits is a work of grace, for you can do nothing to earn any of these blessings. They are simply the fruit of following after me, allowing me to be your Shepherd and lead you.

Beloved, no man or woman can pastor you like this. However, I do raise up godly people to shepherd you in my name. The only shepherds you are to follow are those who in their turn follow me. They can only benefit you in as much as they allow me to benefit them.

I warn against following those hired as shepherds or pastors, who view their responsibilities simply as a job and not a joy. Follow those who follow me, men and women of the Word and the Spirit, who seek to live in agreement with me.

However, beloved, don't make false expectations of them. Don't expect them to supply your needs. Their responsibility is to help you meet with me so I can answer your needs personally. Those who live in an agreement of faith with me can encourage your faith. Those who seek to live in obedience to my word, out of love for me, can encourage you to obey. As men and women of prayer, they can show you how to pray with faith in my name and in agreement with my word. As men and women of the Spirit, they can show you how to flow with the Holy Spirit in your life, and how to honour the anointing I have placed on you.

Yes, because they have such great responsibilities in leading you and caring for your spiritual welfare, you are to give them double honour. **Seek to bless them and make their care of you a joy**. Don't judge or criticize them, or blame them for your own mistakes!

However, beloved, you are not to idolize them either; you are not to allow them to take my rightful place. It is I who am your Shepherd and I who will lead you. You are first and foremost *my* child and *my* disciple!

It is I who give you eternal life so that you will never perish; no man or woman can do that. They can lead you to me, but only I can be your Lord and Saviour, your Healer and Provider. Only I am the Way, the Truth and the Life.

Isaiah 43:1   Psalm 23   John 10:14–16

29

Dealing with Disagreement

He who is not with me is against me.
Matthew 12:30

My beloved, you don't have to try to get yourself into a place of agreement with me. Jesus has already placed you there. You don't have to do anything to be at one with me. Jesus has already done this, and made it possible to live at one with me, enjoying His life and sharing in His work.

Sin is terrible in my sight because it disrupts the agreement between us. When you sin, you are not at one with me. I forgive you when you repent, and this restores you to the place of agreement; again you are at one with me through the blood of Jesus. Can you understand why I want to eradicate sin from your life?

The sins you desire are attractive only to your flesh, not to my Spirit living in you. He is never attracted by sin; it is so awful to me because I had to give the life of my Son to save you from its power.

To agree with me is also to agree that my will for you is better that anything you could desire for yourself. **Jesus never acted in independence. He spoke only my words. He made it clear that He had come to do not His own will, but my will**.

I want you to agree with me that it is better to embrace my will for your life than your own will, better to walk in my way than in any way of your own. When you are self-willed and stubborn I won't stop loving you; but I am not going to change my plan and purpose for your life to fit in with your desires.

Are you willing to deny anything in your life that is not in agreement with me, that is not my will for your life, no matter how much your flesh desires it? The cross you have to carry is not something laid on you that you don't want, like sickness or oppression. No, your cross is that which you willingly take up day by day. **It is the cost to your self-life, to the flesh, of walking in agreement with me, in my way, in my will, in my purpose for your life.**

You have to agree with my estimate of your flesh: there is nothing good about your self-life! Apart from me you can do nothing. There is no point in promoting your self-life, nor in trying to serve me in your own strength. Without faith it is impossible to please me. You need to agree with me about this. Then you see the wisdom of trusting in me rather than in yourself.

Jesus taught and trained His disciples to live in agreement with Him. This is why He rebuked Peter so strongly when he tried to correct Him. Jesus looked at Peter and said: 'Get behind me, Satan. You are on the side of man, not of God.' Jesus was not only rebuking the enemy: He was issuing a harsh warning to the apostle. Satan is opposed to my will and therefore opposed Jesus. He doesn't agree with me, nor will he ever do so. Those who disagree with me side with him. **Those who are not with me are against me.**

Yes, beloved, you are called to agree with me. Is your wisdom greater than mine? Do you have a finer understanding of the truth than I do? Is your will going to be more effective than my will for you? Do you imagine there will be a heavenly reward for those who have opposed me? Do you really imagine I will be pleased with you for fulfilling your aims while opposing my purpose?

I supply all the grace you need to walk with me; but I will not supply the grace to disagree with me! And what desires of the flesh can possibly compare with the life of agreement with me, and all the blessings of my grace that result?

John 8:28–30   John 6:63   John 15:5

30

Overcoming Sin

Can two walk together unless they are agreed?
Amos 3:3, NKJ

My beloved, I have called you to walk with me. How can we walk together unless we are in agreement? It is not for me to agree with you, but for you to be in agreement with me. Sin is disagreement with me; it is alien to my purposes for you or any of my children. So whenever you sin you are in disagreement with me. This affects our relationship, and we cannot enjoy close fellowship and an intimate walk until I have forgiven you.

I don't condemn you for your sin; my mercy is always available to you. I am ready to forgive you as soon as you confess your sins. However, you know you offend me by repeating the same sins again and again. This produces in you a sense of failure and even defeat. There have been times when you have been determined not to grieve me in these particular ways again; yet, although you have been sincere, this hasn't worked, has it? Do you know why, beloved?

Although you agree that your sin is wrong, you still don't agree with me how awful it is. I hate sin and I want you to hate it in the same way! I am not telling you to hate yourself, but to hate sin. You see, beloved, you will avoid what you hate.

Since you were born again there have been significant changes in you and in your perception of what is right and wrong. There are some things in which you indulged yourself in your former life. You don't want anything more to do with them, because you now see them for what they really are; they are awful in my sight, and they have become awful in your sight as well. You are now in agreement with me about those particular things.

But what of the sins that persist? You know these things are not right, which is why you confess them as sins. They persist because you don't hate them as I do, or as the other things from which you have turned away. Even though they are wrong you still desire them, which is why they still have a grip on you.

You have sometimes hated yourself for failing, for yielding to the same temptations again and again. This is not the same, though, is it? If you hate the sin itself, you will avoid it altogether! What does my word say about Jesus? That He loved righteousness but hated wickedness: therefore I raised Him above His companions by anointing Him with the oil of joy.

You see, beloved, when you hate even the idea of sinning and grieving me in any way, this is a joyful thing. Yes, it is good to love righteousness, to do what is right in my eyes; for then you agree with me further and this strengthens our relationship.

Because I am righteous, it is only the righteous who can walk in agreement with me. Unless I had forgiven your sins and cleansed you from all unrighteousness you could not walk with me at all. I want you to be free to enjoy a close and intimate walk with me.

Instead of compromising in those areas where you continue to sin, see how terrible even the smallest sin is to me, for all sin is an offence to my holiness and righteousness. **Instead of hating yourself for failing, hate the sin, so that you will not fail!**

What of those things you really want to put out of your life, the things you have fought to overcome, yet without success? You have made decision after decision to change these areas of your life, but still without success. You have even asked me to help you change, and have felt disappointed when the sin persisted. Because you know I want you to be free of such things – the bad temper, the wrong relationship, the habitual sin, whatever it might be – you have been disappointed that I didn't give you the ability to conquer the problem.

Do you know what the problem is, child? *You* are fighting. *You* are trying to overcome. You ask for my help, but only so that *you* are able to gain victory. But why fight when Jesus has overcome already?

Does this mean you give in to the sin? Not at all! If Jesus has already been victorious, why are you fighting a battle that has already been won? To fight the good fight of faith is to trust in what Jesus has already done for you! Victory is my gift to you through Him, another aspect of my grace. But you cannot appropriate that gift by faith while you are still trying to gain the victory yourself.

Why not be honest and admit that there is absolutely nothing you can do to overcome the problem? Yes, stop fighting and start believing! Pass the problem over to me; I am able to change things rapidly once you yield yourself to me and believe that I have given you the victory. Does this seem unreal? Try it. Stop fighting in your own strength and believe I give the victory through the Lord Jesus Christ! Thank me that you are more than a conqueror, because you overcame without having to do the battling!

Hebrews 1:9   Romans 6:1–2   Romans 6:11

The Spirit of Truth

*But, when he, the Spirit of truth comes, he will guide you into all
the truth. He will not speak on his own; he will speak only what he
hears, and he will tell you what is yet to come. He will bring glory
to me by taking from what is mine and making it known to you.*
John 16:13–14

My dearly beloved child, my Spirit who lives in you always
wants to bring glory to me. He does this in your life by taking
what is mine and making it known to you. There is no other way
to receive revelation of the truth of who I am and what I purpose
to do in your life. Without such revelation, you can only depend
on your own human understanding, which is never perfect.

To live by the truth is the way to live in freedom. This is not
the truth of how you (or anyone else) see things; but of how the
Spirit of truth reveals them. Deception comes when you think
you know what is true, but are wrong. What you believe has not
come from revelation through my Spirit of truth, but from your
own understanding, by listening to your own feelings or human
intelligence. I am not anti-intellectual. It is simply that my truth
is beyond reason. No one can think their way to God or into my
favour.

Are not my thoughts higher than your thoughts, and my ways
greater than your ways? My Holy Spirit will never limit your
thinking, your understanding or your faith. No, He will expand
all these things. He will increase your understanding of the
truth. He will stretch your thinking.

Some imagine that to believe the revelation of scripture is
evidence of being small-minded. How wrong they are! When
you believe what I say, your thinking is expanded beyond the
limits of human reason. It requires faith to believe that all your
sins are forgiven on the cross, that you are blessed now with

every spiritual blessing in heaven in Christ your Lord, that you are able to do the same things as He did, and greater things still. It is only big-minded people who think in terms of the miraculous.

Listen carefully, beloved. **Although my Spirit lives in you, He doesn't speak from Himself. He speaks only what He hears**. He is in perfect harmony with me in heaven. He is my mouthpiece to you. He is the One who gives you my counsel. He listens to me and declares what I am saying to you. He is the Spirit of truth, so He will always lead you into the truth. He will never deceive you.

Some of my children become confused because they mistake their own thoughts and ideas for the voice of my Spirit. They sometimes listen to deceiving spirits who want to cause confusion and indecision within them; they want me to speak about a particular matter, but listen to themselves instead. Being impatient, they are not prepared to wait on me for the revelation they need.

Most of their mistakes come from trying to force me to make a decision at the wrong time. They want me to agree with their plans. Sometimes they become frustrated with me because I don't give them the answers they need, when I know they are asking the wrong questions.

I know not only what to say, but also when to reveal my purpose to you. My timing is always perfect. I have impressed on you how important it is to honour the presence of my Holy Spirit within you, and not to grieve Him in any way. The more you live in harmony with Him, submitting to being led into all the truth by Him, the easier it is to hear His voice, and your awareness of the discernment He gives will be more acute. You will heed His warnings and be obedient to the way in which He leads you.

Remember to leave the initiative in my hands. Faith responds to what I say and does not take the initiative away from me. You are following me, beloved, I am not following you. Don't you think I know what is going on in you? Don't you realize that I understand your circumstances? I know what you need to hear, and when. I won't be rushed by you or anyone else! Nor am I ever late. And I certainly don't forget about you!

All my children like to know what lies ahead of them in the future. My Spirit will tell you things that are to come. However, He will do this only at my prompting, when it is important for you to know what lies ahead. He is your spiritual 'eyes', to show you the way to go *now* as well as in the future.

I don't want you to treat the Holy Spirit as some kind of divine fortune-teller. Leave it to me, and to my timing, to tell you what lies ahead of you. There is no point in having vision for the future if you don't know what I am asking of you today. I live in you *today*. You live in me *today*. I want you to live in close fellowship and harmony with me *today*.

So understand, beloved, that my Holy Spirit will guide you into the truth *today*. He will listen to me and declare to you what my heavenly will is for you *today*. He will bring glory to me by taking what is mine and making it known to you *today*. My future plans for you will unfold as you allow Him to lead you step by step. He will not only show you the way, but will enable you to walk faithfully and obediently in it.

Isaiah 55:8–9   John 16:13–15   Ephesians 4:30

32

My Holy Spirit

*But just as he who called you is holy, so be holy in all
you do; for it is written: 'Be holy, because I am holy.'*
1 Peter 1:15–16

My beloved, my desire is that you should be holy. Holiness is not
something for you to fear or avoid, but to embrace. To walk in agreement
with me is to agree with the Holy One. The blood of Jesus has
made you holy so you can be at one with me, your Holy Father.

Holiness is not something beyond you; I have already placed
the Spirit of holiness within you to enable you to live and walk in
holiness. If this is my objective, it has to be yours also; or we are
not in agreement. **It is holy to agree with me, unholy to disagree!**

What does it mean in practice to be holy? Jesus lived the
perfectly holy life on earth. Was He miserable? No, He was the
man of joy, a joy that raised Him above His companions. So holiness
is not being long-faced, having all the joy taken out of life.
Quite the opposite. Being holy causes you to be full of joy.

Was Jesus boring? Of course not! It was exciting to walk with
Him, to see the life of my Holy Spirit working through Him,
transforming lives, healing bodies, setting captives free from evil
and bondage. So a holy life is not a boring life: it is full of the
supernatural activity of Jesus.

To be holy is to be full of love, as was Jesus; full of power and
authority; full of grace and mercy. It is living in the fullness of life
Jesus came to give you. It is living a life that is pleasing to me;
yes, living in right relationship with me. It is agreeing with me,
not only in what you believe, but in the way you live. Holiness is
not simply the absence of sin; it is living the positive life of my
Kingdom here on earth.

My Spirit of holiness wants to be expressed in your life, for He
enables you to live the Jesus life. **He cannot be expressed in sin**.

This is why you need to agree with me about how awful sin is; it cuts right across my purpose for you.

Jesus cannot be expressed through unbelief. The holy life is a life of faith in the Holy One. So you see why it is important for you to agree with my Word.

Jesus cannot be expressed through disobedience. Holiness is expressed in obedience to my will, and therefore to my Word.

Jesus cannot be expressed through your flesh-life, but only through my Spirit within you. The reason why some are afraid of the very idea of being holy is that it is a threat to their flesh-life. **A clear choice has to be made: whether it is your intention to walk in the flesh, seeking to please yourself and fulfil your own selfish ambitions; or whether you will agree with me, walk in the Spirit and seek to fulfil my will for your life**.

Unholiness is a contradiction to my purposes and doesn't belong in the lives of my children. It never pleases me to see any of my beloved ones being complacent about the unholy aspects of their lives. I have sanctified you in Christ. This means I have set you apart for my purposes. You don't belong to yourself. I purchased you with the blood of Jesus, for my purposes to be fulfilled in your life.

It is not a matter of trying to be holy; you could never accomplish this. Jesus is your holiness. You live in Him. You live in the One who is Holy, and He lives in you. You are at one with the Holy One because you have been cleansed by His holy blood. I want you to express the life you have already in Christ, that life I have placed in you by my Spirit.

My apostle Peter urges his readers to be holy in all they do, and he was a man of action. He understood that holiness is practical. To live a holy life is to live full of the power of my Spirit, doing the things Jesus did. Agree with me that this is not only my will for you, but it is made possible by my Spirit who lives in you. Don't disagree with me. Agree, beloved!

1 Corinthians 1:2   Ephesians 1:4   Ephesians 5:25–27

33

The Fruit of the Spirit

But the fruit of the Spirit is love, joy, peace, patience, kindness,
goodness, faithfulness, gentleness and self-control.
Galatians 5:22–23

My beloved, the fruit of the Spirit are the qualities of my life that the Holy Spirit will cause to grow in your life. They were all evident in the life and ministry of Jesus, and therefore are all aspects of a holy life.

Jesus came in love and demonstrated that love, even to the extent of allowing Himself to become the atoning sacrifice for the sins of the whole world. He loved people – His disciples, the multitudes who followed Him, even His enemies who put Him on the cross. My holiness is expressed in love, and so, because I have called you to live a holy life, I want you to love people.

Jesus was the man of joy. He demonstrated that to live a life in perfect agreement with me is to live a happy, contented life, so joyful that His joy raised Him above all those who were around Him. And this despite the continual pressure, opposition and rejection He experienced! Do I not tell you to rejoice always and to give thanks in all circumstances?

Jesus lived in perfect peace because He lived in perfect submission to me and obedience to my will. He was able to impart peace to others, therefore. When you live in harmony with me you are at peace, even in the most trying situations.

Jesus exhibited patience. He waited patiently for thirty years before the time was right for His ministry to begin, even though He was surrounded by so much need during that period. He patiently taught and nurtured His disciples; even though they were sometimes slow to understand what He said. Will you be patient with others, as I am with you?

Jesus expressed His loving kindness in the ways in which He was merciful. In mercy He forgave sins, He healed the sick, He taught the people and He met their practical, physical needs, even if it required miracles of His grace to do this. For example, He multiplied the loaves and fish so that the people would not go away hungry. Beloved, the merciful are blessed; and I want you to be blessed! Need I say more? Don't be like the unmerciful servant, who was forgiven much but refused to forgive the paltry debt of his fellow servant.

Jesus overcame evil with His goodness. He was tempted in every way, yet never yielded to temptation. He lived the sinless life so He could be the Lamb without blemish, the sacrifice that would make all who believe in Him spotless and sinless in my sight. Is this not my word to you, that instead of complaining about evil, you overcome evil by doing good?

Jesus had a humble and pure heart. Instead of judging and condemning people, which was His right, He sought to restore them to my purpose. He lived to serve, without any selfish motive of His own. He didn't seek His own glory, but wanted to glorify His Father who sent Him. See yourself living such a life!

Jesus proved faithful in all I asked of Him. He never disobeyed me, but lived in perfect agreement with me. He spoke the words I gave Him to speak, and did the things He saw me doing. The more you are sensitive to my Spirit, the more possible this will become for you.

Jesus had perfect self-control, preferring my will to His own, even when experiencing the great agony in the garden of Gethsemane. He could stand silent before the false accusations against Him at His trial. Beloved, you don't have to defend yourself against unrighteousness; I vindicate my righteous children. I will act for you!

The same Spirit that was in Him is in you, beloved, to reproduce those same qualities of life in you. No amount of striving will make you more loving or gentle or kind. It is not a matter simply of desire, but of co-operation with my Spirit.

Often your natural life urges you to be selfish instead of loving, to be full of self-pity instead of being full of joy. Your flesh causes conflict with my Spirit instead of peace. You are naturally impatient, and sometimes you hurt others by your words instead of expressing my mercy and loving kindness. There are occasions when you judge and condemn instead of being merciful.

Instead of goodness, you sometimes choose sin; instead of living faithfully, there are times when you say one thing but do another. You are gentle with some but harsh with others, and on occasions indulge yourself instead of denying yourself. So my Spirit has quite a job on His hands to change you into my likeness, with ever-increasing glory.

However, He is not daunted by the task. He is well experienced in doing this in multitudes of people who are very similar to you. But you can either hinder or help Him.

Your agreement with me encourages the life of the Spirit within you. To disagree encourages the life of the flesh that is in direct opposition to the life of my Spirit. And this always produces conflict within you instead of peace. When you agree with me, more of the life of Jesus is expressed in and through you. I like that!

These qualities are not only what I want to reproduce in you; you want an increase of them yourself. And others will be thankful the more they see more of these qualities in you. If you possess these qualities in increasing measure, they will keep you from being unfruitful and ineffective in your witness and the ministry to which I call you.

Ephesians 5:8–10   John 14:9   Ephesians 2:14

34

The Gifts of My Spirit

Therefore you do not lack any spiritual gift.
1 Corinthians 1:7

My beloved, earnestly desire the spiritual gifts. Don't be content with those you have already seen manifested. Be eager to use all the gifts that are available to you.

Do you need to receive a word of wisdom? My Spirit will give you this. Do you need a word of knowledge, of revelation, that will help you understand a particular situation? My Holy Spirit will supply such a word.

Do you need my Spirit to give you the gift of faith, when you find it difficult to agree with what I say? He will do this also.

Do you need to receive healing, or to be an instrument of my healing grace to others? Again, my Spirit is your enabler. He can work miracles through *you*.

You can use the gift of prophecy to be my mouthpiece to others. However, test everything to ensure that all you say is completely in line with my word. Don't accept anything that contradicts the truth of scripture, for that has certainly not come from my Holy Spirit.

You are able to distinguish between spirits, for my Holy Spirit will enable you to sense when someone else is speaking or acting in obedience to my Spirit. When someone speaks from their own soulish perspective or is being used by the enemy, their deceptive words and actions may sound or appear good, but the witness of my Spirit within you can show you that something is wrong.

Beloved, those who speak in tongues edify themselves. For when believers use this gift, they allow the Holy Spirit to pray in them, through them and for them. It is always good to let God Himself pray for you! My Spirit always knows what to pray, even when you don't. And He always prays with faith; He would never pray with unbelief. So this is an important gift to use.

When used publicly it should be coupled with the gift of interpretation so that everyone present might be edified. You see, beloved, it is always the intention of my Spirit to build up and encourage my children, not mystify them!

Walking in the flesh, listening to your own thoughts and ideas, dulls you to the voice of my Spirit. Walking in disobedience, ignoring the warnings He gives you, has a similar effect.

If you walk in agreement with me then you will become increasingly alert to His voice, and quick to respond to what He says. He is always working for your good. He lives within you, not only so that you will know my will, but to enable you to fulfil it.

You have an anointing from God. Treasure that anointing!

1 Corinthians 12:7–11   1 Corinthians 14:12   1 Corinthians 14:1

35

Your Anointing

But you have an anointing from the Holy One.
1 John 2:20

*As for you, the anointing you received
from him remains in you.*
1 John 2:27

Beloved, no one can anoint themselves. I call you by name; I choose you; I anoint you with my Holy Spirit. I myself impart this precious gift to you, the guarantee of your inheritance to come. You can rejoice that no one can take this gift from you, not even the devil himself!

Don't waste this precious gift. It saddens me that some rejoice in the wonderful experiences they have when receiving my Spirit, but don't appreciate *why* I have given them this anointing.

The anointing of the Holy One is to enable you to be holy in all you do. What does it signify if a child of mine thanks me for the experience of my Spirit, but then walks in wilful disobedience to my will? When a believer imagines that the experience of receiving my Spirit takes him or her beyond the need to heed and obey my word, that person is deceived. My words are the truth, and my Spirit the Spirit of truth. The two belong together and are to work together in your life. **The Holy Spirit enables you to live my word, not ignore it!**

This anointing teaches you all things, teaches you to hear and obey my word to you. Jesus lived His message. **I call you as my child to speak the gospel to others in the power of the anointing I have given you, and to live the message you proclaim. You are a witness of the truth, not only by what you say but through the things you do; they are to be a visible demonstration that the truth is alive and at work in you. Then**

not only will you be set free by the truth, but others will also be set free because you will influence them with the truth.

It frustrates my purposes if all my children want to do is enjoy themselves, without living the life I enable them to live by the anointing of my Spirit and doing the things I call them to do. You don't want to add to that frustration do you, child? You want to please me, don't you? To fulfil my plan and purpose for your life?

This is why I explain what you are able to do through the anointing of my Spirit. I want to enlarge your vision to see the possibilities that are opened up to you through living in agreement with me. I want you to be a doer of my word, not a hearer only! I have not placed my Spirit within you for you to deceive yourself by hearing but not doing what I say.

Because of the anointing you have received, you are able to do not only the same things as Jesus but greater things still. Does this seem wrong to you? Impossible? Blasphemous, even? Well, beloved, it is Jesus Himself who said this of anyone who believes in Him. Don't be deceived and believe the falsehood that says this is impossible for you! You need to understand what Jesus means.

He said that anyone who had faith in Him would do greater things still 'because I am going to the Father'. When He returned to heaven, He promised to ask me to pour out the Holy Spirit on those who believed. This happened at Pentecost when the believers were gathered together; the Spirit came with wind and fire upon each of them.

What was the result? When they prayed and ministered to others, the Holy Spirit came upon them, too. To receive the anointing of the Holy One is the greatest thing that can happen to you or to anyone. But this could not happen while Jesus was on earth; His Spirit lived in Him and was not given to all freely until He had returned to the glory of heaven. Then this greatest of all gifts could be imparted to all who believe.

Because you have received this anointing, you can impart it to others in my name. You can pray with them and the Holy Spirit will come upon them. Of course, beloved, this is not an excuse to become proud. All the glory and honour goes to me, for you are able to impart to others only what you have freely received as a gift through my grace.

1 John 2:27   Isaiah 61:1–2   Psalm 45:2

36

Do Not Grieve My Spirit

And do not grieve the Holy Spirit of God, with
whom you were sealed for the day of redemption.
Ephesians 4:30

My beloved, there have been times when you have grieved my Holy Spirit. You haven't listened to what I have said and you have failed to heed the warnings I have given you through Him. You have always regretted this afterwards, haven't you?

You see, beloved, because He wants to guide you into the truth, He wants to save you from unnecessary failure, conflict and even defeat!

However, you grieve Him by failing to listen to what He says, or failing to take heed of His warnings. **Any sin grieves Him, for He is the sinless One living within you, able to help you withstand all temptation and keep you from sin.**

However, you don't stop to think what He would consider right in your situation. There are even occasions when you invite sin into your life, by deciding to do what you want, without any reference to the Holy Spirit.

This always causes conflict and sorrow afterwards. You see, beloved, if you don't obey the leading of my Spirit then you either follow your own inclinations or listen to the evil one. Both the flesh and all the powers of the enemy oppose the working of my Holy Spirit. So anything in your life that is not holy grieves my Holy Spirit. It is just as well that I am so gracious and merciful, isn't it? For I don't take my Spirit away from you because you disobey Him or fail to heed what He says to you on my behalf. Patiently, He waits to restore you.

The more aware you are of the presence of my Spirit, the more readily you will sense when you have grieved Him. And you will feel this grief deeply because you have failed, have been disobedient or have yielded to temptation.

It is at this point that the devil will try to make you feel falsely condemned. He will suggest that you are a useless failure and that you will never be able to overcome in the weak areas of your life. He wants you to think I am ready to wash my hands of you, because you have sinned and failed once too often.

Sometimes he may suggest that you have grieved me so deeply that there is no way back into my grace, that the only appropriate way for me to deal with you is to punish you. He is a liar, of course, the father of lies. So don't believe any of his suggestions.

There is an important difference between the grief resulting from grieving my Spirit and the condemnation the enemy wants you to feel. My Spirit's aim is to encourage repentance so you can be restored. The enemy's aim is to make you feel defeated and incapable of restoration.

Every day you can avail yourself of my mercy and be forgiven. Then the conflict caused by grieving my Spirit is replaced by a renewed sense of peace. Again, you can be profoundly thankful for my grace, that I don't treat you as you deserve, and never separate you from my love or from the flow of blessings I want to pour into your life.

Beloved, it is so important, therefore, not to delay when you know you have done something to grieve me, whether minor or significant. Put things right with me immediately. Don't allow the enemy to gloat over you. His schemes are undone by the power of Jesus' blood that cleanses and lifts you out of condemnation.

So, beloved, be thankful for every work of my mercy in your life. And remember to be merciful to others!

Romans 8:1–2   John 16:7–11   Isaiah 35:8–10

37

The Fruit of Agreement

Do not believe me unless I do what my Father does.
John 10:37

My beloved, because of the unity and the complete agreement between us, Jesus could say: 'The Father and I are one.'

His complete obedience and submission to me came out of His love for me. And so, beloved, Jesus made it clear that those who love Him would be obedient to Him; they would keep His commands. Obedience was the evidence of Jesus' love for me, and your obedience will be the evidence of your love for Him. Love for me is not having sentimental feelings for me, but living at one with me, in agreement with me, and therefore in obedience to me.

Jesus obediently laid His life down by dying on the cross. If at any point Jesus had disobeyed me, or even acted independently of me, He would have sinned and there would be no possibility of salvation for you or for anybody else. So you see how fruitful His obedience has been! Multitudes will enjoy eternity in heaven, living in my glory and total acceptance, because of His obedience.

You cannot see the fruitfulness that will come from your obedience to Jesus. Remember, my plan for your life is that you bear much fruit, for this is how I will be glorified in and through you. And I give you this assurance: **if you obediently follow the leading of my Spirit you will be fruitful. He will never tell you to do anything that doesn't work; neither will He lead you on a course that will result in failure**.

The way to continue to live in that love is through obedience: 'If you obey my commands, you will remain in my love, just as I have obeyed my Father's commands and remain in His love.' You see, beloved, I want you to live in my love, to abide, remain, continue in that love, by obeying Jesus, by living in agreement with Him. So don't be afraid of this word 'obedience'. It is simply the fruit of living in agreement with me and allowing my love to be expressed through your life.

If you have such a wonderful inheritance through my grace, why is obedience so important? Because when you are not in agreement with Jesus you are not able to avail yourself of all those riches that are yours in Him. Unbelief on the one hand and disobedience on the other prevent you from living in the good of the inheritance that is yours in Christ. This is why my servant Paul says that **the only thing that matters is faith working through love. That combination of faith and love keeps you in agreement with Jesus, and therefore with me**.

Your obedience does not earn anything from me; but it does enable you to live in the flow of my grace; and from the fullness of that grace you will receive blessing upon blessing.

How do you know when you are living in the agreement of faith and love, expressed in your obedience to Jesus? You are full of joy! Jesus said, when speaking of obedience that comes from love for Him: 'These things I have spoken to you that my joy may be in you and that your joy may be complete.'

Do you not see that this is what I want for you? A life full of joy! A life in which you experience the fulfilment of knowing you do my will.

Am I too demanding? No; but it is true that of those to whom much is given I require much. I don't want my gifts wasted, but used for my glory. Because I have enriched you in every way. You have certainly received much.

All I ask of you in return is that you agree with me. Live by faith in Jesus, rather than in yourself. Live in loving obedience by loving others as He has loved you. The idea of obedience is not enough; it has to be outworked in practical ways.

John 10:17   Galatians 5:6   Luke 12:47–48

38

How to Love Me

I love those who love me, and those who seek me find me.
Proverbs 8:17

My beloved, love desires a response of love. I want you to declare your love for me, not only in words but in what you do. Those who love me want to please me; they do what I command. They know that obedience is not expressed in empty words, expressions of love for me that find no substance in their lives.

You see, beloved, I know your heart. I even know every thought that passes through your mind. I know when you want to please me and when you are motivated by selfishness. The greater your love for me, the greater your obedience, for true love for me is expressed in agreement with me, in submission to my will.

Many of my promises are linked to obedience to my word. **You do what I say; I do what I promise!** To the faithful I prove myself faithful.

I am not speaking of a slavish, legalistic obedience or a begrudging acceptance of my will. No, true obedience comes from true love for me. Do you want to please me? Do you want to show that your love for me is not empty words but true love, expressed in seeking to do what I say?

When you want to please me, I show you what to do; and I am right there with you, ready to help, enable and encourage you.

You see, beloved, I don't hide my presence from those who want to know me. Those who seek me find me. Neither do I hide my riches and resources from those who need them in order to obey me. I am right there with them, the Lord who is ever present.

Beloved, you can tell those who truly know me, for they express their love for me in the obedience that is demonstrated in their lives. I am Love; so any who know me know my love. That draws from them a response that is expressed in obedience.

Do you know any disobedient believers, those who have little or no regard for my will? How well do you think they really know me? A superficial response to the gospel is the evidence of a superficial relationship with me. Your closeness to me is demonstrated for all to see by the person you are and the things you do: the deeper a believer's relationship with me, the more wholehearted their obedience. The one flows automatically from the other.

You can see why my servant John says that those who claim to love me but don't do what I say are deceived and the truth is not in them. They may know the truth, but it is not being expressed in their lives.

I am glad you want your love for me to be real and to be expressed in a life of obedience lived for my glory. The rewards for obedience are immense; those who love me are not motivated by reward, but by a desire to please me. Everyone wants to please those they genuinely love. I am so hoping that you want to please me, beloved disciple!

John 14:15   John 14:23   1 John 3:21–24

39

Grace to Do My Will

Lay hold of my words with all your heart;
keep my commands and you will live.
Proverbs 4:4

It is a matter of the heart, isn't it, beloved? The nature of *your* heart. There are times you want to hear my voice, to know what I am saying to you, but there are other times when you would rather not listen to what I say. You are afraid I might interfere with what you want to do!

It is never wise to try to avoid me or what I want to say to you. In doing what I want, you find fulfilment, peace and joy. You experience a sense of freedom and the ability to enjoy life to the full. But seeking your own way instead of mine produces conflicts within you. Tension develops in your relationship with me and you are no longer at peace, because you are no longer walking in agreement with me. When this happens I don't stop loving you, nor do I cause the river of my grace towards you to dry up.

However, before you can enjoy the full flow of my blessings, I wait for you to come round to my way of thinking. I await a change of mind and heart. I will not submit to your will, so you have to humble yourself and submit to me.

Sometimes this is not so easy. Not because I make it difficult; but you can be a very stubborn child when you want to be! You can stubbornly resist my will for you, even when my purpose is to bless you.

Of course, there is no future in such an attitude. However, there are times when you still choose to please yourself instead of me. These occasions become less frequent as you discover the value of obedience.

You don't like that word 'obedience', do you, my beloved? You think that I want to restrict your freedom, when the very opposite is the case! Did not Jesus die to set you free? Does not the presence of my Spirit within you mean that I want you to be free?

Yes, you are free from the things that restrict and inhibit you. You are free to obey me, free to follow in my way. When you choose your way rather than mine, that is not freedom; it is placing yourself back under the restraints of your flesh. Your flesh-life will only restrict you. True liberty is expressed in obediently following the leading of my Holy Spirit.

Those who think that because I am gracious obedience is unimportant are sadly mistaken! **I have made all the riches of my grace available to my children to enable them to do my will**. I give them the grace to obey, not as a compensation for deliberate disobedience. Yes, my dear beloved child, I will give you the grace to obey me lovingly and graciously by submitting your will to mine, denying yourself, taking up your cross daily and following me.

Don't repay my love for you by being foolish and unwise, by disregarding my word and doing whatever pleases you. Am I not your Father, your Creator, who formed you for my own purposes, who called you and set you apart for my own pleasure? When you see me face to face I want to be able to say to you: 'Well done, good and faithful servant, enter into the joy of your Lord.'

Matthew 25:14–30   Matthew 28:18–20   1 John 3:21–24

40

My Purpose

The LORD Almighty has sworn, 'Surely, as I have planned,
so it will be, and as I have purposed, so will it stand.'
Isaiah 14:24

Beloved child, some of my people are so proud they imagine they know better than me. They consider their plans to be better than my purposes for them. They fight against my will, even though they say they love me. They forget that I called them for my purposes.

Beloved, I have made you with free will. I make my will clear to you in my word, but I never force you to obey me.

Others look around them and are perplexed, for they see so much happening in the world that is inconsistent with my will and purpose. They come to the conclusion that things are out of my control. This is never the case. I have created humankind with the ability to seek me and find me, to know me and discover my will. Because of their sinful natures, instead of loving me and one another most grieve me by taking advantage of one another, causing hatred, division, war and strife, violence and all kinds of abominable sins.

I give them time to repent before they have to face judgment, which will be the time of reckoning. For then they will be confronted with their failure to fulfil my divine purpose. Those who have obeyed me will not need to fear, for they will be released into the joys of my Kingdom, for which they have longed. But for those who have opposed my will it will be a time of fearful judgment.

I will not need to condemn them. On that day they will see for themselves that their evil deeds have condemned them already. They will see clearly who I am and that I deal with absolute justice.

Can you not see that you and others who know me need to use every opportunity to make my love and grace known to others? Everyone needs to hear that I am ready to save them from the condemnation they deserve and to welcome them into my Kingdom. They can trade darkness for light, condemnation for loving acceptance, unrighteousness for faithful obedience!

You see, beloved, people can make their own plans, but it will be mine that will prevail in the end. Meanwhile, don't be surprised at the violence and ungodliness in the world around you. This is humanity manifesting its fallen nature. Humanity without God perpetrates the works of the devil. It is only to be expected. However, I will have my way in due course.

Meanwhile, it is important that I have a people for myself, a people who will demonstrate the life of my Kingdom in the midst of all the unrighteousness and ungodliness of the world. Beloved, I have called you to be one of those people.

I am not hard-hearted, but I am firm. This is why I tell you clearly that I will not change my plans for you, or for anyone. It is for you to embrace my plans for your life, not for me to embrace your plans!

What I do in you as an individual I do among my children generally. I must have an obedient people. I am not speaking of obedience in attending services and meetings, saying and singing fine-sounding words only to go and live as the world lives rather than demonstrate the nature of my Kingdom on earth.

Righteousness is the sceptre of my Kingdom. If, therefore, you are going to live the life of my Kingdom here on earth, you will need to be righteous in the way you live, doing what is right in my sight. In the midst of the world's turmoil I need you to demonstrate my peace and joy. I want you to point others to me, so they see that I alone can save them from the violence, hatred and pain the world and the devil inflict upon them. I, and no other, can save them! I want them to see from your example that my Kingdom is righteousness, peace and joy in the Holy Spirit.

It is not my purpose that unrighteousness shall prevail. I sent my Son to rescue my people, and all who put their trust in Him are saved from the condemnation they deserve. There will be a new heaven and a new earth. The former things will pass away and my Kingdom will be fulfilled. Those who love me will reign with me without all the negativity of the world, the flesh and the devil that seems to be so prevalent at present.

I will surely do *all* that I have said I will do. It shall be as I have declared it shall be. My purposes for my creation will surely be accomplished. And this includes my purpose for *you*!

Romans 6:16–18   Mark 1:14–15   John 5:24

41

Beware of the Deceiver

I, the LORD*, speak the truth; I declare what is right.*
Isaiah 45:19

My beloved, to walk in the truth is to walk with me in the power of my Spirit. I am not like the enemy who lies, deceives, accuses and condemns. I am He who wants to save, heal and see my people set free.

Those who believe my word are kept from being deceived by the evil one. Even though he is the deceiver of my brethren, he cannot take away from you the life I have given you, but he can prevent you from living in joy and freedom if he can persuade you to believe his lies. He cannot condemn you, because I have saved you from condemnation; but he can encourage thoughts of false self-condemnation that rob you of your confidence and faith. His aim is to persuade you that you are incapable of doing my will and merit only my disfavour and judgment. He fails to remind you that all my purposes are fulfilled by grace and that you are a child of grace.

You can do whatever my word says you can do. You have what my word says you have. You will become what I have planned you should become, one who reflects my glory and has been transformed into my likeness.

Don't doubt my ability to bring to fulfilment everything I have planned for you. Why devote your life to working for food that spoils? Work for the food that endures to eternal life, that I give you. Why store up for yourself treasures on earth, where moth and rust corrupt and thieves break in and steal? Why not store up for yourself treasures in heaven, where there is no corruption and no one can steal your inheritance from you?

So don't be deceived by any of the devil's lies. He will suggest you cannot truly be seated in heavenly places with me. He is jealous because he has been thrown out of heaven! He will tell you that you cannot possibly live in agreement with me because your sin disqualifies you. He wants you to believe that your false feelings of condemnation prove that the blood of Jesus has not really atoned for your sins, that you are not forgiven and cannot possibly be at one with me.

The enemy knows that the truth is so powerful that he has no answer to it. Therefore his tactics are to try to undermine your faith in my word, for then you will not live in the agreement with me that Jesus has made possible. Don't allow yourself to be deceived.

When you believe what I say, you have the life, the love, the power, the healing, the freedom of which my word speaks!

Matthew 6:19–21   James 1:22   Matthew 7:21

42

Avoid Deception

I am the LORD, *and there is no other;*
apart from me there is no God.
Isaiah 45:5

My beloved, I am *the* Lord of heaven and earth. My plans shall be fulfilled, for I am the final authority! There is no other god or spirit that can compare with my authority and power.

I did not create humanity to be evil, disobedient, unrighteous. I made men and women in my own image, to live in fellowship with me, to be in perfect harmony and accord with me. Yet when people rebelled, they became destructive, and their hearts became set on pleasing themselves instead of me. Having yielded to the temptations of the devil once, it became their nature to do so again and again.

I didn't create spirits to do evil, to oppose my will. When Lucifer fell, many fell with him. Whoever opposes me cannot prevail, for I am the final authority; I am the only Judge of the living and the dead. All will have to give account to me and come under my judgment.

You have nothing to fear, beloved, because you are a child of my grace. Through that grace I have made you a co-heir with Christ of my heavenly riches.

I sent my Son to make salvation available to all who turned to Him with repentance and faith. Can you see how important it is, therefore, to make Him known to those who are under judgment? They need to know that my love and grace are available to all who come to me with repentance and faith. Even if they choose to reject the truth, they still need to hear of my offer of salvation.

Because the devil is a deceiver and the father of lies, many have become deceived. Some think their own goodness or their own deeds can save them, despite the unforgiven sins in their lives. Even though they have disregarded me, they imagine I will welcome them into heaven, as if they had earned this by right. They have no idea of their need of my mercy and grace.

Others have looked to deceiving spirits, thinking that other spiritual forces will save them. They believe the lies of these spirits and therefore hate Jesus and all He stands for, even though He alone is the true source of salvation.

The commission I have given my Church is to go into all the world and make disciples of Jesus. Disciples know and believe the truth. By my grace they have been saved from the condemnation they deserve. They love me and want to obey my commands, including this great commission to make Jesus known to others. There can be no compromise; whatever is not of the truth is false. Stand firm, therefore, against all that is false. **Hold fast to the truth with all your heart.** Those who hear my word but choose some other course of action deceive themselves. I don't want you to be deceived by what is false, neither do I want you to deceive yourself. Believe my word, act upon it and walk in the truth! As you do so, you will be a witness to others who need to know me, a witness to my love, my grace and my truth.

Luke 10:18–19   Luke 8:15   Romans 8:17

43

My Plans for You

'For I know the plans I have for you,' declares the LORD,
'plans to prosper you and not to harm you, plans to give you
hope and a future.'
Jeremiah 29:11

My beloved, sometimes you seem perplexed and confused about my plans for you. On occasions you are discouraged because it is apparent that things you experience couldn't possibly be my best purpose for you. At such times you don't know what to think or which way to turn. You wonder, even, if I am really in control of the circumstances that affect your life.

The plans I have for you are good; I want you to prosper. It is never my purpose to harm you. That is the desire of your enemy, the one I have overcome for you.

I call you to be a child of hope, to see all my wonderful promises to you fulfilled, to know that your future destiny is safe in my hands. I want you to prosper in all I call you to do. I tell you to seek first my Kingdom and my righteousness and then *everything* else will be added to you. As your Shepherd and Provider, I don't want you to lack anything.

Why does this seem so extraordinary to you? Am I not your Father? Have I not made you a co-heir with Christ? How can you believe this and imagine I desire anything evil for you? Sometimes you may experience ridicule and rejection by others because of your faith. But I have not planned such things; they are the inevitable cost of being faithful to the One who was continually rejected. Did not Jesus warn that if they hated Him, they would hate those who believed in Him?

You know my future plans for you in heaven are good! I am your Father and Shepherd while you are on earth as well as for all eternity. You don't have to wait until you go to heaven; I have planned good things for you while on earth. There is reward here on earth as well as in heaven for your faithfulness to me.

There is no conflict between grace and reward. I have made it clear that all the blessings you receive are given through my grace. However, I do also make it clear that everyone will be rewarded now and eternally for what they have done.

You can't earn my blessings, but you do reap what you sow. If you sow love, you will reap love. If you sow joy, you will reap joy. If you sow mercy, you will reap mercy; if you sow provision, you will reap all the provision you need, and more!

Even in the way I reward you my grace is at work. For I always give back more than you give: good measure, pressed down, shaken together and running over! Your salvation, giving you access to heaven, is my gracious gift to you. Your place in heaven will be determined by what you have done, how faithful and obedient you have been to my will. Do you not remember that Jesus made it clear that each person will be rewarded according to what they have done? Heaven is my gift to you; your place in heaven is your reward!

I have made you righteous, and the righteous shall live by faith. In order to accomplish what I call you to do, you need to trust me. I will never fail you nor leave you to your own devices if you trust in me. **I make the plans, I determine the purpose and I give you the faith to see my will fulfilled.** However, you have to exercise that faith, to put it into practice day by day. Your willingness to live by faith will reap a reward now and eternally.

Will there be opposition and difficulties? Inevitably! I have warned you that in the world you will have tribulation; but be of good courage, for I have overcome the world. Yes, beloved, my plan is that by trusting me you will overcome whatever opposition and difficulties arise. Those who overcome will receive the crown of life.

The problem for some of my children is this: they think that these difficulties are my will for them. So instead of rising up in faith to overcome them, they passively accept them. This distorts their whole understanding of who I am. What kind of father would plan such evil things for his children? Certainly not me!

I wouldn't have sent Jesus to take all your burdens on Himself and then deliberately cause you to have those burdens. This is like saying I want you to sin because He has made it possible for you to receive forgiveness. Such a suggestion is outrageous!

On the cross Jesus overcame all evil powers, so that by trusting in Him you can overcome all the difficulties and opposition you encounter. Don't think of these problems as my plan for your life. See yourself as an overcomer, not someone who passively accepts everything that happens as my will.

I tell you to rejoice in the trials you have to face, because these demonstrate that your faith is genuine. As your faith is in me you will always pass the test, for I will never fail you! I will enable you to overcome the trials so you can enjoy the rich inheritance I have given you.

I have a positive plan for your life. I have prepared good works for you to walk in.

I have not planned sickness, pain, distress for you. I have given you a Saviour, a Healer, a Provider, a Shepherd to free you from such need.

He is my plan for you. So live in Him and let His words live in you; and you will prosper, beloved child! Let me say this again: **Jesus is my plan for your life,** that you might know Him, love Him, serve Him and possess all the riches that are in Him, and have a rich reward in heaven!

Ephesians 2:10   Proverbs 16:3   Proverbs 16:9

44

Fear Not

Do not be afraid, for I am with you.
Isaiah 43:5

My beloved, there is no need for you to fear. Fear is a *natural* reaction in certain circumstances. Faith is the *spiritual* reaction! It is your flesh that fears, not your spirit. For I have not given you a spirit of fear, but of love, power and a sound mind.

There is little point in trying to analyse your fears. What you truly want is to overcome the fear. Take your eyes off yourself, for the nature of your flesh cannot change. Focus instead on my presence and know that no matter what the situation I am with you.

You certainly do not need to fear my future plans for you. What I ask you to do in my name I don't expect you to accomplish alone; so you do not need to fear failure.

My beloved, what is the point of my being with you if you forget I am with you, or don't take advantage of my presence? If, instead of trusting me, you attempt to do things in your own strength, you will inevitably fear failure when confronted with things that seem too great for you, or problems you wish to avoid but cannot. It is natural to fear, for you cannot overcome in your own strength. But you have my supernatural presence and resources available to you. It is a matter of choosing where you are going to place your trust, in yourself or in me. Don't say you are unable to trust me, or cannot overcome those fears! It is a matter of choice. Listen to your faith, not your fears!

How can you believe that I am with you, and still be afraid? How can you believe that you live in me and I in you, and still be afraid? Don't you believe that my perfect love casts out all fear?

Why do the fears persist? Remember what I taught you about your soul and spirit. There is no fear in your spirit, only in your soul. The problem begins in your mind. You react negatively to your circumstances. Your emotions are the product of the way you think. If you think fear, you feel fear. That fear will then paralyse you into inactivity. You will feel you cannot do what is placed before you, that you are totally incapable of coping with the situation.

You can see that this is your soul acting independently of my Spirit. In other words, your fear is a reaction of the flesh. Ministry cannot change your flesh! You need to change your focus.

Beloved, my grace is sufficient for you. It is at the very point of your weakness that you can discover my strength. When you feel under pressure, look to me and praise me. Don't forget the blessings and benefits that are yours because you are my beloved.

Remember what my servant David said:

Praise the LORD, O my soul;
*   all my inmost being, praise his holy name.*
Praise the LORD, O my soul, and forget not all his benefits,
*   who forgives all your sins and heals all your diseases,*
who redeems your life from the pit
*   and crowns you with love and compassion,*
who satisfies your desires with good things,
*   so that your youth is renewed like the eagle's.*

Beloved, these things are true for you too. What David said to his soul, you will often need to speak to your soul! **When you feel afraid begin to praise me, for this will take your eyes off yourself and help you to focus on me and all I have done for you through Jesus:**

- **I forgive all your sins.**
- **I heal your diseases.**
- **I redeem your life from the pit of condemnation and destruction.**
- **I crown you with my love and compassion.**
- **I satisfy your desires with good things.**

Fear has to do with punishment. It is my purpose to love you, not punish you. And there is no fear in love. None of the negative experiences you have experienced were punishment from me. Jesus died in love for you to save you, not punish you. So praise me for your salvation and live every day in the knowledge of my love for you, the perfect love that casts out *all* fear!

When you praise me you are exercising your spirit where there is no fear. When you look at the flesh, all the fears come crowding back! Praise puts your focus on to the One who has overcome and will enable you to triumph.

2 Timothy 1:7   1 John 4:18   Romans 8:15

45

I Am Your Rock

You are my Father, my God, the Rock my Saviour.
Psalm 89:26

My beloved, it is a great privilege to have me for your Father! I have chosen you for this honour because I have a destiny for you that can only be accomplished through knowing me and having a close relationship with me.

Sometimes you tell me that you love me, but you don't want to listen to what I have to say to you! You are not still long enough in my presence to hear what I want to say. Even when I want to assure you of my love, you have the habit of shutting your ears to my voice and listening to your feelings instead.

I have already shown you how practical my love is. During His ministry, Jesus didn't go around speaking loving sentiments to the people. In love He healed the sick, delivered people from evil, forgave their sins and taught them the truth that would set them free. He came with the gift of my Kingdom and demonstrated the power of that Kingdom. Love in action!

I give you assurances of my love for you; the most effective assurances, however, are not my words of endearment but what I do for you.

I understand you and know all about your circumstances. I always have the right word to speak to you, the word that will build faith, keep you in hope and will give you the direction you need. So listen to me! Faith comes from hearing my Word proclaimed to you through my word and by my Spirit.

I am working out my plan and purpose, even when you cannot always understand the direction in which I am leading you. As your Father and God, I always have your own best interests at heart. **In all things I am working for your good, because you love me and have been called according to my purpose.**

Your fulfilment will be found in accomplishing the plans I have for you; any other course you take will only lead to ultimate frustration.

This is why you have to forsake your own plans for mine. There is no point in having any secret agendas, for you cannot hide them from me. I know when you are sincere about my plans for you, when you earnestly desire to know my will and to obey me, because you want to please me and bless me.

I myself am the Rock, the same foundation on which your life is built. Follow my word, believe what I say and put it into action, and you will not be shaken. Depart from my ways and you become vulnerable to the attacks of the evil one, whereas in me is total security. Choose a course of your own and you have to look to yourself to accomplish what you want to do. That is never wise, and has produced problems in the past, hasn't it, my beloved?

Remember what Jesus taught: the foolish man, whose house was built on sand, heard the word but did not put it into practice. The wise man's house was built on rock, because he not only heard the word but did it. When the storm came his house stood firm, whereas the house on sand fell. I want the best for you because I am your Father. My love for you is sure and certain; it doesn't change with circumstances. It is the steadfast, sure and certain love that is like my word: utterly reliable and dependable.

I don't mind how much you depend on me, for I am your Rock, your Saviour. As you trust me, I not only lead you forward in the way I want you to go, but I save you from all and any who would seek to prevent you fulfilling my purpose for you. So you have no need to fear!

Romans 10:17   1 Samuel 2:2   Psalm 92:15

46

My Saving Power

I am your salvation.
Psalm 35:3

My salvation will last for ever, my righteousness will never fail.
Isaiah 51:6

My beloved, I have saved you from a life without me, from the hands of the enemy, from your sin, failure and disobedience. I have saved you for myself so that now you belong to me. I am jealous for my own; so I guard you and keep you.

My work of saving grace in your life continues every day. I save you from danger, from the destructive power of the enemy, who wants to steal, kill and destroy. I save you from making grave mistakes; I lead you through my Word and my Spirit, wanting always to keep you walking in my ways. Whenever you listen to his voice, I save you from falling into temptation and impending danger.

If you sin I forgive you – again and again. When necessary I restore you, build you up and encourage you. I enable you to walk in the way I set before you, in harmony and fellowship with me.

All this is evidence of the fact that I am your Salvation. You see, beloved, salvation is a process, a relationship with me. I have saved you, daily I continue my saving work in your life. And I will save you on the day when you appear before my throne of judgment. You will still need my saving grace at that time. However, you can be confident that because I have saved you for myself, I will save you from judgment on that day. Yes, beloved, I will surely do that, for it is not my intention, having claimed you for myself, to lose you. By grace I will enable you to inherit the place I have prepared for you.

If it is by my grace that you have been saved, then you need to continue to live in the good of my grace day by day. For those who have proved faithful to me there will be a rich reward in heaven. Have I not promised that all shall be rewarded according to what they have done? Salvation is my gift to you: your reward the fruit of your obedience to my will for your life.

So you see, beloved, it is important that you don't treat your salvation lightly or take it for granted. It is not right to think that, because I have saved you, it doesn't matter how you live now. Nothing could be further from the case.

I haven't saved you so that you can live a life of independence or rebellion. I haven't saved you to persist in a life of sin and disobedience. No, I have saved you to walk in righteousness all the days of your life, to know me, to live at one with the One who is your salvation.

Don't think of salvation as something you have or haven't got, or as something you can keep or lose. This is to misunderstand the nature of my salvation entirely. **I am your salvation**. I want you to live a 'saved life' in relationship with me. It is such a relationship that is a gift of my grace, a relationship in which you will continue to live by my grace and that you will be able to enjoy eternally in heaven because of my grace!

Isaiah 51:6   Psalm 27:1   1 Peter 1:3–5

47

Is Anything Too Hard for Me?

I am the LORD, the God of all mankind.
Is anything too hard for me?
Jeremiah 32:27

Let's get this settled once and for all, beloved child! Is anything too hard for me? I created the earth and everything in it. *Is anything too hard for me?*

When I sent my Son to the earth, He healed the sick, He overcame the devil and the power of evil, He even overcame death. He raised others to life and was Himself raised by me. So I ask you, *is anything too hard for me?*

I am He who parted the Red Sea, fed my people with manna in the wilderness, pulled down the walls of Jericho. *Is anything too hard for me?*

I made Saul, the arch-persecutor of my Church, into the great apostle of the nations. I called fishermen to be my disciples and made them the founding fathers of my Church, that has prospered and grown throughout the countries. I ask you, *is anything too hard for me?*

I save people from hell, heal them from cancers and deliver them from the curses of witchcraft and the occult. I ask you, *is anything too hard for me?*

So why doubt my power in your life, my ability and willingness to meet your need by the power of my mighty arm? My prophet spoke my word: 'Who has believed our message and to whom has the arm of the Lord been revealed?' You see, my beloved, whenever people believe my word and the promises I give, the power and majesty of my might are revealed.

I want to raise the level of expectation among my people; you can see that. And I want to do this in you, my beloved! You have a rich and powerful Father who loves you and so is always willing to provide for you, to help you and to meet your need.

Of course, as a loving Father I don't spoil my children. I teach them to be responsible and obedient, for I love those who love me; I hear their cry and I answer them.

Instead of thinking of your smallness when you pray, think of my greatness – the greatness of my love for you, the greatness of my resources. The more you consider my greatness, the more you will realize that your smallness doesn't matter very much. One as great as I am can certainly care for one as small as you!

Matthew 19:26   Luke 1:37   Mark 14:36

48

Don't Limit Me

Now to him who is able to do immeasurably more
than all we ask or imagine, according to his power
that is at work within us …
Ephesians 3:20

My beloved, is it your walk that concerns you? Your track record since you became a believer? Well, I forgive all the failure of the past as soon as you ask me to do so! And I supply sufficient grace to enable you to keep walking with me in faithful and loving obedience.

Have you not availed yourself of that grace? Have you tried to walk in your own strength instead of my power? You don't need to continue like that, do you? I have placed my Spirit within you. You have my divine power within you, as I keep reminding you! So you don't have to resign yourself to a life of failure in the face of temptation.

Within you are the resources of my love. You can love anyone I give you to love. I have given you my wisdom so you will know what to say and do, how to express my love to them. I have given you my power so that you can convey to them the life of my Kingdom.

It saddens me when my children have my resources within them but settle to live at a level far inferior to that which is my best purpose for them. They close their ears to my word and the voice of my Spirit, and settle for so little. They have such a small concept of my love. They don't believe I would give them much or do anything great in their lives, and don't expect me to work to bless others.

If a father lived on the edge of poverty but bought his son a birthday gift costing £10, that would be a great gift to that child, and a considerable sacrifice for the father. However, if a millionaire gave a similar gift his child would think nothing of it, and such a gift would be of little consequence to a rich parent.

Beloved, is not the wealth of the nations mine? Does not the earth and all that is in it belong to me? Am I not richer than all the millionaires put together? Are not the resources of my spiritual power so great that I was able to bring all creation into existence?

So why expect so little of me? Why think that my Spirit within you could accomplish so little? **I want to see you set free from small-mindedness when it comes to the things of my Spirit. I want to free you from a poverty mentality concerning what I am prepared to give you and do for you. I want to free you from unbelief concerning the way I want to work in and through you by my Spirit!**

I know that apart from me you can do nothing. But you do not want to live apart from me! Nothing is impossible for the one who trusts in me. I have brought you this far in your walk with me, through many difficulties and traumas, and I will lead you on.

Always expect the future to be better than the past, the blessings to be greater as you learn to trust in my grace more and more. I am changing you into the holiness of Jesus with ever increasing glory. Within you is the mind of Christ, and He is neither small-minded nor poverty-stricken in His thinking.

Mark 9:23   Matthew 23:23   Matthew 18:18

49

A Child of Light

The LORD is my Light and my salvation – whom shall I fear? The
LORD is the stronghold of my life – of whom shall I be afraid?
Psalm 27:1

My beloved, I am the light of the world. I have called you to be a child of light. You don't belong any longer to the darkness. **I have brought you out of the dominion of darkness and have made you a citizen of my Kingdom of light.** Those who follow me don't stumble around in the darkness; they have the light of life.

The thief often acts under the cover of darkness. Satan is a thief; he wants to steal the revelation of light that my children have, and lead them back into the darkness, back into sin and bondage. To turn away from me is to turn away from the light and embrace the darkness. You don't want to do that, my beloved! Some prefer the darkness, for they think it hides their evil deeds. But nothing can be hidden from my sight.

Those who remain faithful to me resist such temptations. The sins of darkness are appealing to your flesh, but not to my Spirit. I hate wickedness and every form of sin. And so, beloved, it is time to rejoice and be glad that I have delivered you from that which offends me. I have cleansed you with the blood of my Son and made you a child of light.

Now you can walk in the light, saying 'no' to sin and temptation and 'yes' to righteousness, doing what is right in my sight.

It is for your own good that I say these things to you. I don't want you to stumble or fall because you have held on to areas of darkness that oppose your best interests and my will and purpose for your life. Darkness not only embraces sin, it causes fear. Those who walk in darkness have no sense of my presence with them; they have lost their vision of my will and direction for their lives.

Some try to have one foot in the light and the other in darkness. This is evidence of a divided heart, of double-mindedness. It produces conflict and confusion in the life of any of my children who seek to live that way.

My beloved, you have made your choice to walk in the light as a child of light. You value your fellowship with me and you know that, because there is no darkness in me, I cannot have fellowship with darkness. If you want a greater revelation of my glory in your life, it is imperative that you understand what this involves. You have to turn away from anything that does not glorify me and embrace that which does give me glory!

You see in the life and ministry of Jesus One who walked perfectly in the light. And you see the consequence of this. When He brought this light to bear on the lives of others, they were delivered from darkness. Their sins were forgiven; they were set free from evil spirits who serve the prince of darkness. They were healed of sickness perpetrated by the evil one, and some were even raised from a premature death.

It is wonderful to know that I have saved you from the darkness in which you once walked, and have made you a child of the light! Turn your back on all that I consider darkness and walk in the light of my truth.

So don't be deceived. The flesh will sometimes be attracted by the darkness because the nature of the flesh never changes. It always wants to please self rather than fulfil my purposes. Being intrinsically selfish, your flesh still wants to sin. This is why it is so important to deny the flesh, to deny yourself.

Remember that in your flesh there dwells nothing good. Absolutely nothing! You cannot please me with your flesh, but only by walking in the radiance of my light as the child of light you have now become. I will give you the grace to do this.

John 10:10   Matthew 6:22–23   John 1:4

50

Live in Agreement with Me

But whoever lives by the truth comes into the light, so that it may be seen plainly that what he has done has been done through God.
John 3:21

My beloved, as a child of the light I want you to walk in the light. This means you will live by the truth. You will live in agreement with Jesus who is the truth, with His words of truth and with the Holy Spirit who is the Spirit of truth.

Jesus is the light of the world, and you are called also to be light for the world. Your light is to shine before others so that they will see your good works and give glory to your Father in heaven. My Holy Spirit is your enabler in all this. In the Sermon on the Mount Jesus teaches what it means to walk in the light, to live as a child of my Kingdom. I want you to understand, beloved, that you can live this way only by living in agreement with Jesus and allowing my Holy Spirit to help you.

You are not to hide the light you have been given. You are to shine that light wherever there is darkness, so that others may see and know the truth.

To live a lawless life is rebellion. Those who break the law and teach others to do so will be called least in my Kingdom. And I want you to be great, not among the least. **The greatest in the Kingdom of heaven are the greatest servants.** Jesus came as the servant of all; that was the measure of His greatness. **To be in agreement with Him means, therefore, that you desire to have a servant heart and are willing to serve my people, even when this is costly.**

To live in agreement with Jesus is not to be angry with your brother or sister, for that makes you liable to judgment. Love them and be merciful to them. If they sin against you, forgive them; don't judge them. If they continue to sin against you, continue to forgive them!

To live in agreement with Jesus is to seek to live in love and unity with others who belong to Him. So, if there is a breakdown in a relationship, you will want to be reconciled. I call you to love your brothers and sisters in Christ in the same way that I love you.

To live in agreement with Jesus is to live in love, not lust. Don't even commit adultery and fornication in your fantasies. Take every thought captive and make it obedient to Christ. Be in agreement with Him in your thought life as well as in your actions. Your mind is often the devil's first line of attack, to plant unbelieving unclean thoughts whenever he can. Keep in agreement with Jesus by being faithful in your marriage and seeking to please Him in all your relationships.

To live in agreement with Jesus is to be a person whose word can be relied upon. If you promise to do something, do it, no matter how inconvenient this may prove to be for you. Then people will know that you mean what you say – like Jesus. You will not make false promises or hide behind tired spiritual clichés. Don't be like those people who like to appear super-spiritual but can never be persuaded to do anything practical. They say they love me, but they are too busy to love their fellows or to lay down their lives for anyone! That is not true spirituality, and one day they will have to account to me for their disobedience. Those who truly love me are obedient. **To live in agreement with Jesus is to give freely and to lend without expecting any return.** You are a steward of all the resources made available to you, including all your finances and property. I entrust them to you to use in the way I direct, as a good and faithful steward.

Wealth makes some people deceitful. It can be the one area of their lives where they refuse to walk in agreement with me. They refuse to obey my word in regard to tithing and offerings. They are deceived into thinking their wealth belongs to them. People with fewer financial reserves often give more, trusting that they will reap a harvest from the seeds they have sown. The wealthy already have barns that are full, so they don't see the need for me or my provision. This is why Jesus said it is so difficult for the rich to enter my Kingdom of heaven.

Understand, beloved, that the agreement of obedience, like the agreement of faith, brings great benefits.

Beloved, when you give, don't announce it openly so that everyone knows what you have given. I am always aware of what you have given in secret, and I will reward you accordingly. I know when you have given what I wanted you to give!

John 8:12   Matthew 23:11   Matthew 18:1–4

51

Seek First My Kingdom

This, then, is how you should pray: 'Our Father in heaven,
hallowed be your name, your kingdom come, your will
be done on earth as it is in heaven.'
Matthew 6:9–10

Beloved child, I want to see my Kingdom come and my will done on earth as in heaven. Because this is my objective, I want it to be yours also: that you live for the cause of my Kingdom.

Those who belong to the world live for a number of causes, often with great sacrifice. **The cause all my children are to live for is to see my Kingdom come and my will done on earth as in heaven.** When you are in agreement with my will, this is the cause for which you live. You cannot pray with integrity for my will to be done in others unless you are concerned to see my will fulfilled in your own life! Pray that my Kingdom, my rule and reign, will be expressed in your life, as well as in that of others; that you will do my will and that others, too, will be obedient.

You are mine; I have paid the price for you. All that you are and have is rightfully mine and is available for me to use for my Kingdom purposes. It is not that I want to take from you; I will always give back far more than you give to me. **But you cannot live in agreement with Jesus without seeking first the Kingdom of God in your life!**

Hypocrites want others to see them praying and giving. The righteous quietly get on with doing what I ask of them, for they are motivated by love, not from some desire to draw attention to themselves. The righteous don't store up for themselves treasures on earth, where moth and rust destroy and thieves break in and steal. They store up for themselves treasures in heaven; they walk in agreement with Jesus, even in the handling of their finances and material resources.

You see, beloved, Jesus teaches a very important principle: that where your treasure is, your heart will be also. I don't want your heart in a bank vault or the stock market; I want your heart to be set on my Kingdom purposes.

Does this mean that it is wrong to have money in a bank or shares? Not if you consider these as assets that belong to me, available for my Kingdom purposes. I can exercise my authority in your life by telling you how to use whatever assets and resources you have. You see, beloved, *everything* in your life is to be in agreement with me. As the King who is on the throne of your life, I want to exercise my reign in *every* area of your life.

What does it say about the nature of your heart if you don't agree with me about the use of your financial and material resources? After all, you want me to bless you in those areas and enable you to prosper. Well, the way to prosper is always to be in agreement with me, the agreement of faith and obedience.

So when you give I want you to exercise faith, to believe you will reap a harvest from the seed you sow. And I want you to be obedient in giving what I tell you to give. My Kingdom will benefit and you will prosper as a result.

Remember, no one can serve two masters. You cannot serve God and money! Let your money serve me and the cause of my Kingdom, and everything will be added to you.

Matthew 6:33   Luke 16:13   Matthew 6:21

52

The New Covenant

This is my blood of the covenant, which is
poured out for many for the forgiveness of sins.
Matthew 26:28

My beloved, I am a God of covenant, and a covenant is a solemn agreement made between two parties. I made a covenant with my people Israel, and gave them the terms of this covenant through my servant Moses. In this covenant I made solemn promises to my people. They, for their part, were to be obedient to my commands; they would then see the fulfilment of what I had promised.

I always remain faithful to my covenant promises. I never break my word. I am faithful in all I say and do. Whenever my people were faithful to their side of the agreement, I caused them to prosper as a nation, as I had promised.

Sadly, again and again they proved unfaithful, especially when I had blessed them so abundantly that many felt they had no need of me. When they were disobedient I would speak to them and warn them of the consequences of their sins. But they paid no heed to the prophetic voices I used to warn them. Time and again I had to use harsher means, not because I desired to punish them, but to bring them back to the place of obedience so that I could bless them, prosper them and fulfil all the covenant promises I had given them.

Whenever they repented and turned back to me I restored them, blessed them and enabled them to overcome their enemies. No sooner had I set them free and caused them to prosper than their compromise and disobedience would set in again.

Do you get the picture, beloved? There were many who simply wanted to use me. Yes, they turned to me in times of desperate need, but wanted nothing to do with me when they felt no need of me!

When my people repented, they came back to the agreement I had made with them. They agreed that they had sinned in breaking the covenant and cried out to be restored. Being faithful to my side of the agreement, I always had mercy on them and restored them. However, this endless pattern of restoration followed by renewed disobedience had to be broken.

I promised through my prophets a new covenant, a better covenant that would be even more wonderful for my people, so great is my love for them. I sent my Son to the world, to establish the new covenant. The conditions of this agreement are different from the old. It was clear from the record of my people Israel that people would never be able to sustain obedience to me, so selfish is the nature of the flesh. So I had planned to do something more radical and far-reaching.

Under the terms of the new covenant I would place the gift of my Kingdom within those who were part of the new covenant. I would give them a new birth, a new life – a new heart, even! All their former sins would be forgiven, and I would place my own Spirit within them to enable them to fulfil their part of the covenant agreement.

Under this new covenant the people are to put their faith in my Son, Jesus, and all He has done for them. They could not be made acceptable in my sight by their own deeds under the old covenant; so now it is possible to be accepted, but only through what He did on their behalf.

Under the old covenant the people failed to obey me again and again; under the new I placed within them the power that would enable them to obey my own Holy Spirit.

When He became man, Jesus did what no other has done. He lived in perfect agreement with me, in perfect obedience to my commands. He fulfilled the first covenant in order that the new covenant might be established. He made this clear. He had not come to destroy the law I had given my people to live by as their side of the covenant. No, He had come to fulfil it!

He could do this only by living in perfect obedience to all that I asked Him to do. This is why He made clear that He had not come to do His own will, but the will of the One who sent Him. With the former covenant fulfilled, He could then, at the end of His time on earth, establish the new covenant.

A covenant has to be ratified or sealed with blood. The old covenant had been ratified with the blood of animals sacrificed on behalf of the people; the new covenant was ratified through the shedding of Jesus' own blood. He became the perfect sacrifice offered on behalf of the imperfect, the sinless life offered for sinners, the Righteous One giving His life for the unrighteous.

Who belongs to the new covenant? Those who repent of their sins and put their faith in Jesus as their Lord and Saviour. They see that through what He did on the cross they are forgiven and made perfect in my sight.

You are part of the new covenant, beloved. Under this covenant you are to live a life of faith in Jesus, so that His life becomes your life, His righteousness becomes your righteousness, His holiness your holiness; yes, even His perfection your perfection.

You see, beloved, there can be no imperfection in the Kingdom of heaven; so it was necessary for me to provide the sacrifice that would make you holy, perfect and blameless in my sight.

The wonderful news is this: **you are already part of this new covenant. I already see you as holy, perfect and blameless because you are in Christ.** As a sign and guarantee of this, and of your inheritance, I have placed my Holy Spirit within you.

Beloved, you are a child of the new covenant, sealed with the blood of Jesus. I will care for you, love you, bless you and bring you to your eternal home in my presence. You, for your part, will live by faith in my grace. You will live in the agreement of faith and obedience, not in your own strength, but through the power of my Holy Spirit within you. He will bring you to the fulfilment of my covenant plans for you.

1 Corinthians 11:25   Hebrews 8:6   Hebrews 8:10–12

A Good Heart

See to it, brothers, that none of you has a sinful,
unbelieving heart that turns away from the living God.
Hebrews 3:12

My beloved, you are greatly blessed to have been chosen by me to be part of this new covenant and to know that I will always prove faithful to my side of this covenant.

Yes, the promises of the new are better than the promises of the old. **For under the new you inherit everything that Jesus inherits; you are a co-heir with Christ. Under the new you have eternal life, my life. Under the new you are in my Kingdom and my Kingdom is in you. Yes, all the riches and resources of my Kingdom are yours in Christ.** Could anything be more wonderful?

So you don't have to earn your way to heaven, but simply to live in that place of agreement with me into which Christ has already brought you through His grace poured out for you on the cross. You see, beloved, **under the terms of the new covenant or agreement, I have already met every need of yours in Christ. Yes, everything that is in Him is yours! Everything!** It is not my purpose to withhold anything from you.

Jesus and those He makes holy through His blood have the same Father. So He is not ashamed to be known as your Brother. Isn't that amazing? That the one who gave His perfect life as a sacrifice for you has become your Brother!

As your Father, I know He will accomplish everything necessary in you to bring you to glory. You see, beloved, you already belong to me and I don't intend to lose you.

However, I do call you to live in agreement with Him, and therefore with me. This is why it is so important that you do not repeat the errors of the old covenant and turn away from me, especially when you feel in no particular need.

Sin hardens the heart. You only have to yield to the flesh a little and it will want more and more. One act of disobedience can quickly be followed by another and another. Although you are part of this wonderful new covenant with Christ in you, you are still able to sin. I don't strike you down dead in judgment, nor do I throw you out of my Kingdom! I continue to bless you and to be true to my covenant promises, don't I?

In other words, it is still easy to sin, and when you do it appears you get away with it. The trouble is that your sin damages your relationship with me, and when you don't take disobedience seriously you are at the top of a very slippery slope. If you are not careful, you will fall from that place where, in unity with me, you are able to receive the gifts I pour into your life. **I don't remove the blessings from you; you remove yourself from the blessings.** I don't remove my presence from you; but in your sin and disobedience you don't want to live in the good of my presence. As with Adam and Eve, when you sin you feel ashamed in my presence and want to hide from me. The fault is with you, beloved, not me!

You see, sin not only hardens your heart so that you no longer want to please me, it also deceives you. You don't see it for the terrible thing it is, damaging the image of my Son in you. When you treat sin lightly, you only regard it as unfortunate and excuse yourself by saying that no one is perfect.

But in Christ you are made perfect. That is why He told you to be perfect as your Father in heaven is perfect. You don't have to try to make yourself perfect or see perfection as an impossible goal to attain. I have made you perfect through the blood of Jesus. This is your starting point now. By my grace I want you to resist temptation, to please me by being obedient to me. You can live a life of agreement with me, if you so choose. Why not thank me that in Christ you have been made perfect, instead of listening to your natural mind that thinks such a thing would be impossible?

I know there will be times when you will fail and I will have to forgive and restore you to the place of perfection that is yours in

Christ. But it is always your heart attitude that concerns me. I want you to have a heart that desires to please me and to live in agreement with me. Then whatever failings you may have, or sins you commit, they will not be deliberate acts of wilful disobedience which are rebellion against my authority.

Beloved, I want you to have a heart after my own heart, thankful that you are in covenant relationship with me. As I will always be faithful to you, so you, for your part, desire above all else to be faithful to me.

Hebrews 10:14   Psalm 51:17   Psalm 86:4

54

Draw Near

*Let us draw near to God with a sincere heart
in full assurance of faith.*
Hebrews 10:22

My beloved, I understand your weaknesses, for Jesus faced the same temptations you face. He had to be completely identified with you so that His life could be a valid sacrifice offered on your behalf. In dying for you He has opened up the way for you to come boldly before my throne of grace, where you will find mercy and all the grace you need to help you, no matter what the situation.

You come to my throne through His blood, through what He has done for you, not through any merit of your own. Being cleansed by that blood makes you entirely acceptable in my sight. You can come boldly, in full assurance of faith; for by His sacrifice on your behalf you have been brought into agreement with me.

Jesus had to be obedient no matter what He suffered. You, therefore, can always be obedient no matter what I ask of you, for I have given salvation to all those who obey me. That is a scriptural truth some want to avoid! They don't understand that, under the new covenant, obedience is still required of my people, the obedience that is the expression of genuine love for me, not the slavish obedience to religious laws and traditions.

I want you to inherit by faith with patience everything that I have promised. **You see, beloved, under the terms of the new covenant, I have put my law in your mind; I have written my commandments on your heart so that you can obey them.** They are not simply words in a book.

Jesus' blood has purified your heart from the works that lead to death; now, together with me, you can perform the works that lead to life.

Beloved, you have access into my heavenly presence because you are one with Jesus. Don't hold back. Come right into the holy of holies where you can meet with me.

See yourself with the eyes of faith, the eyes of your spirit, standing now before my throne. The host of heaven worships me, giving me the honour and glory due to my name. And there you are in the company of the redeemed, with my name written upon you. See yourself bowing in worship before my throne, humbly acknowledging my Sovereign Lordship over your life.

Beloved, we can have fellowship together before my throne. You don't have to wait until you die for this communion. Jesus has opened up the way for you *now*. This is the measure of the grace I extend to you, of the love that draws you ever closer to me.

Don't disagree with my word or deny the privilege I have given you. Agree with what I say, and come!

I will speak with you, strengthen and encourage you. I don't draw you close to judge you. Whenever you draw near you will know my mercy and grace. And, beloved one, I will send you from my throne to fulfil the destiny to which I have called you.

Hebrews 2:18   Hebrews 4:15   Hebrews 12:1–3

55

No Need to Worry

Therefore I tell you, do not worry about your life.
Matthew 6:25

Beloved child, why worry? What does it accomplish? Worry is like saying that the problem is too big for me, as your Father, to handle, so you will worry about it instead! Is this not absurd?

Because you are my beloved child I take a keen interest in all your affairs. I am aware of all your circumstances and needs. In my love, I want to provide and help you. Agree with Jesus when He says that I, your heavenly Father, know your needs. I know what lies ahead of you tomorrow and on every subsequent day. I promise to give you all you need for today. Tomorrow I will do the same, and on the next day the same. There has never been a day when I have failed to supply what you have needed. Because I want you to walk in close relationship with me, I supply on a daily basis. This is why I tell you not to worry about tomorrow; each day brings with it enough concerns. **I will give you faith for today. Tomorrow you will have faith for the challenges tomorrow brings, and the grace to meet those challenges.**

I am He who gives food at the proper time. I open my hand and satisfy the desire of every living thing. Even in the midst of famine I provide for those who trust in me. That is the promise of my word, and I watch over my word to perform it.

You cannot agree with Jesus and worry! If you agree with Him you will trust Him, no matter how dire the circumstances may appear to be. Worry is an absence of faith, not an expression of trust.

You may say that it is natural to worry. Yes, that is the reaction of the flesh to trying and difficult situations, but it is not the reaction of your spirit. And I am teaching you to walk in the Spirit, not the flesh; to live in faith, not fear. And worry is a form of fear!

If I can provide for the animals, the birds and the other aspects of creation, then I can certainly provide for you, the pinnacle of my creation. For I have created you in my image and made you my beloved child, a co-heir with Christ. To worry is natural; to trust because you agree with Jesus is spiritual and opens up the reservoir of my supernatural resources. If you live in agreement with Jesus, He is able to touch every area of your life and supply according to His riches in glory, no matter what the nature of your need.

You don't need to be envious of others, either. **No one is as rich as the one who lives in agreement with Jesus!** No one has greater riches available to them, and these are eternal riches. Neither do I want you to be jealous of the way I have provided for other brethren. They have access to the same source as you. You have the same Father, the same Lord, the same inheritance. You, too, are a co-heir with Christ.

Don't compare yourself with others. Look, rather, to me. I am the only one who can satisfy your need. Much more will be accomplished by looking to me in agreement of faith than worrying!

Your mouth gives you away, beloved, for it is from the overflow of your heart that your mouth speaks. If you live in agreement with Jesus, you don't speak negatively about your circumstances, therefore. You do not complain, grumble, moan or appear dissatisfied. No, beloved, you see things as Jesus sees them.

Is this easier said than done? It may seem like that to you, but only because you are not accustomed to agreeing with Jesus and seeing the circumstances of your life as He sees them. When you pray, entrust things into His hands and leave them there! Don't keep taking back the problem and trying to work out the solution for yourself. Speak with faith over your life. Instead of speaking about the problem, speak the solution that I have made possible through Jesus.

Matthew 6:31–33   Luke 12:11–12   Luke 10:41

56

Don't Judge

*Do not judge, or you too will be judged. For in the same way
as you judge others, you will be judged, and with the measure
you use, it will be measured to you.*
Matthew 7:1–2

My beloved, I have entrusted all judgment to Jesus. You are not
the judge; He is.

Yet when He came to earth, He didn't come to judge but to save.
Instead of implementing the condemnation humanity deserved,
He gave His life for them to save them from that judgment.

Yes, He will come again. And when He does so, it will be to
judge. Meanwhile you live in the period of mercy and grace,
when all humankind is given the opportunity to be saved from
the judgment deserved by all, by putting their faith in Jesus and
the power of His blood that will cleanse them from their sins and
make them holy and acceptable in my sight.

Every day you live in the saving grace of Jesus. Every day His
mercies are available to you so that you can be cleansed from
anything and everything that does not agree with Jesus. You need
to be continually thankful that you are a child of my grace and
that I am always extending my mercy and forgiveness to you.

**Because I am merciful I expect you to be merciful. Because
I am gracious I want you to be gracious.** Those who walk in
agreement with me will reflect my mercy and grace. If I choose
not to judge and treat others as they deserve, then, as you walk
in agreement with me, I don't expect you to judge or treat others
as they deserve. I am very strong about this. I make it clear that
whenever you judge others, you place yourself under the same
judgment you have placed on them. That is not a clever thing to
do. Jesus died to save you from judgment; why place yourself
back under it?

You judge another for the speck in their eye. I see *all* that is not yet fully in line with my will in them, yet I don't judge them. If you could see all that was wrong with others, you would find it very difficult not to judge them. That is because you are not as merciful as I am. If you judge them for the specks in their eyes, what would you do to them if you saw all that I see?

Why don't I judge them? For the same reason I don't judge you: I can see them in Christ, covered with His cleansing blood. If that is how I see them, this is how you are to regard them!

Judgment is an attitude of the heart that condemns people for what they are or the things they do. I don't want any such judgment in your heart, beloved.

However, I do not intend you to suspend all your critical faculties, for I warn you to be aware of false prophets, of wolves who come in sheep's clothing. You can judge whether a person is acting in my name or not by the fruit they bear. Using the discernment of the Holy Spirit to judge right from wrong, the good from the bad, is different from having a wrong heart attitude of judgment towards others.

My word is like a sharp double-edged sword. It cuts to the division of soul and spirit. It shows what is of humanity and what is of the Spirit. Both my Spirit and my word will enable you to have right discernment. This doesn't give you the right to judge, even those who are the perpetrators of evil. You can hate the sin but have to love the sinner. Do I not tell you that you are to love even your enemies? If you were to avoid all who are instruments of the devil, or all those who have evil hearts, you would have to leave the world altogether.

Those who are not with me are against me. That was true of you once; you were against me, you didn't live in agreement with me. It is only by my grace that you have been saved and that I am teaching you now to live and walk in agreement. So don't judge those who are still in darkness. Pray for them. Be a witness of the light to them. Show them my love, even if they do throw it back in your face. When they do, show them the other cheek and go on loving them.

And when you see a brother or sister in the faith fallen from grace, seek to restore him or her instead of judging and gossiping about the situation. And if you see another believer in disobedience or unbelief, clearly not in agreement with me, don't judge that person. Pray for them, and ask me to show you if there is anything you can say or do that will help that person come back to the truth.

One thing is certain: people will not want to receive help from you if they think you are judging them. They will be very much more open to receive from you if they know you are motivated by love, not judgment.

Luke 6:37   Romans 14:10   1 Corinthians 4:15

57

Right Attitudes

*Not everyone who says to me, 'Lord, Lord,' will enter the
kingdom of heaven, but only he who does the will of my
Father who is in heaven.*
Matthew 7:21

Beloved child, I have impressed on you how important it is for you
to live in agreement with me, and that this agreement is expressed
both in faith and in loving obedience to my will and purpose.
Jesus makes it abundantly clear why this is so important.

I have saved you to do my will on earth and then enjoy your
heavenly reward. I have not saved you for your own purposes,
but for mine. Nobody comes into agreement with me by simply
calling me 'Lord'. Neither are they necessarily living in agreement because they have received wonderful experiences of my
Holy Spirit.

Because all judgment belongs to me, you don't have to judge
who will be in heaven and who will not. I alone am the Judge. It
is for you to live in the good of my saving grace, to use the
resources of my Spirit I have given you, so you can do what I ask
of you and bear much fruit for my glory.

Remember, the wise build their house on the rock; they hear
my word *and* put it into practice. The foolish hear what I say but
don't do it. Consequently, when the storm comes their house
falls; for it is founded on the sand.

You see, beloved, the rock is not simply my word, but *doing*
my word. **The one who puts my word into practice walks in
agreement with me and is able to withstand any storm, no
matter how fierce.**

Some think they can choose what to believe in my word and
reject the rest. Who do they think they are? What do they think
they are doing? This is the pride and independence of the flesh.

Their trust is not in me, but in a religion of their own making where they each set themselves up as the judge and the final arbiter of what to believe. Do they really imagine they can be saved from judgment by creating their own religion and statements of faith? Do you think they can please me by choosing what to believe?

There is a difference, beloved, between someone who is ignorant, or even deceived, and someone who has rejected the revelation of truth and has chosen to walk in their own way instead. Their life is certainly founded on the sand. It is foolishness of the highest order to oppose the revelation of truth I have chosen to give through my Son.

It is not enough for a person to say that they believe in Jesus, or even to say that He is Lord. Those who truly believe in Him believe His words. And those who believe His words seek to be doers and not hearers only of these words.

You cannot see anyone else's heart, but you can tell what is in their heart from the things they say and by observing their actions. This is not an invitation to judge, but it is wise to know who your companions are. Just as you can only walk with me by agreeing with me, so you can only walk in unity with others who are in agreement with me. The unity between you will come from the common faith and obedience you share.

You cannot walk together with those who have the form of religion but not the life of my word. Neither can there be unity between those who call me Lord, yet do not walk in my way or live to fulfil my will.

It may sometimes seem that there are relatively few who truly want to walk in the agreement of faith and obedience. Don't be discouraged; I have a history of doing great things through relatively few. Jesus left only a handful of believers behind when He returned to heaven, but look at what has happened since! From those few, countless millions around the world have been saved.

You see, beloved, where there is true unity I command the blessing. Jesus prayed that you might be one with me, just as He and I are one, and one with other believers so that the world will know that I sent Him, that He is the Son of God, and that people will also see that I love you in the same way that I love Jesus. He prayed, therefore, that you live in agreement with me and with others, so that corporately you will be a witness of faith and love to the world.

Don't use the anointing I have given you for your own ends, doing in my name things I have never asked you to do. Keep your heart right and your motives pure. Stay in agreement with me by walking in faith and being a doer of my word.

Matthew 7:24–27   John 17:20–21   Romans 15:5–6

58

Your Food

*'My food,' said Jesus, 'is to do the will of him who sent
me and to finish his work.'*
John 4:34

My beloved, Jesus made it clear that His food was to do the
Father's will and to finish the work for which I had sent Him
to earth. Your food is the same, therefore: to do my will and to
finish the work to which I have called you.

Listen, beloved: I am not saying this is your duty or even your
responsibility; it is your food. Food nourishes you, giving you the
necessary energy to live. Spiritually, doing my will feeds you,
providing the necessary energy and motivation to be fruitful.

Jesus also said that the work of God is to believe in the One He
has sent. So your food is not to do good works for me, but the
works that come from faith, from your agreement with me: those
things I tell you to do.

A royal official came to Jesus because his son was desperately
ill. Jesus told him: 'You may go. Your son will live.' The man took
Jesus at His word and departed. While still on his way home he
received news of the boy's recovery – and at precisely the time
Jesus had told him that his son would live.

Do you see the significance of this? **The man took Jesus at
His word**. The official believed what Jesus said and acted upon
His word. This is what I ask of you, beloved, for this is when you
are truly fruitful. Hear what I say through my word and by my
Spirit, and act upon it.

This is your food, child. Stop listening to voices that contradict my word and take heed of what I say.

Just as Jesus could do nothing by Himself, neither can you. He
did whatever He saw me doing, and I want you to do whatever
you see Him doing. You see, you cannot be in agreement with me

and act independently of me! The two concepts are completely contradictory. In my love for Him I showed Jesus what I was doing in every situation, and in my love for you I will do likewise for you.

You don't have to begin with grandiose ideas about my purpose for you. Always remember that those who prove faithful in little things are put in charge of much greater things. Prove faithful in the small things I ask of you, and then you will prove trustworthy in greater matters. Don't despise the small beginnings. Stephen began by waiting on tables, then became the worker of great miracles, signs and wonders that he performed in my name.

You see, beloved, whatever I ask of you or send you to do can always be accomplished in the power of my Spirit. I wouldn't send you to do something you couldn't do through faith in me. I don't lead you in failure. I know all my children and their abilities. I always choose the right person for the right job. You don't see things that way, do you? Sometimes you thought I was mistaken in selecting you to do certain things you felt incapable of doing. You failed to understand that I was developing the faith I know you are capable of exercising. To do this, you had to be in a situation where you could do nothing other than trust me!

You see, in the same way that I sent Jesus, He sends you. He came in my name to do my will. **You are sent in His name to do His will.** Just as I enabled Him, so I will enable you. I will never fail you as you put your trust in me.

I didn't send Jesus to fail, but to accomplish whatever I wanted Him to do. **He doesn't send you to fail, but to bring light where there is darkness, hope where there is despair, healing where there is bondage to evil, revelation where people are blind to the truth, faith where there is unbelief, love where there is fear, and encouragement where people are discouraged.**

Listen, beloved, there are people in need around you. They need me, and they need you because you are sent in my name, the one who can take my love, my life and my power to them. And whatever you do in the name of Jesus will prosper!

Every day by my Spirit I am directing millions of believers, ensuring that the right person is in the right place at the right time, ready to be used to touch the lives of others with my love and power. Again and again you will find that the way has been prepared for what you have to do. Every day I place people before you that you can love and serve. You don't have to imagine that seeking my will is going to be difficult, or that you will only know what you are to do after a prolonged period of prayer and fasting. No, beloved, begin with those I place immediately before you. I will give you the words to speak and show you what to do, if you are sensitive to the leading of my Holy Spirit.

I am with you always; when I send you, you don't go alone. I am always at hand, ready to help, encourage, direct and reveal my presence in that very situation. You will see by the way things work that I knew exactly what I was doing when I sent you!

Yes, my sheep hear my voice and follow me. They do what I say and the hungry are fed, the thirsty are satisfied. The stranger is made at home, the poor are clothed, the sick are comforted and even the prisoner rejoices that someone has brought light into the darkness.

This doesn't mean that I expect you to fulfil the need of everyone you meet; that would be impossible. No, be sensitive to my Spirit and He will show you what to do.

John 6:27   Luke 8:50   Matthew 8:8

59

In My Name

For I did not speak of my own accord, but the Father
who sent me commanded me what to say and how to say it.
John 12:49

My beloved, whenever you go to others in my name, my Spirit will tell you what to say and how to say it. He is the Spirit of wisdom and will give you exactly the right words to speak, even when you are completely perplexed about the situation that confronts you.

It is much more effective to be my mouthpiece, because I am speaking through you, than to try to counsel others with your own spiritual knowledge. With only a few words Jesus dealt with major problems. His spiritual knowledge exceeded yours by far, yet He didn't speak from His own spiritual knowledge but used the words I gave Him to speak. This is why His words proved so effective. When people came to Him He didn't examine them about every area of their lives, neither did He lecture them or even preach sermons at them. He spoke the words that would bring release and victory into their situations.

You see, beloved, the few words I give you will be far more effective than many words of your own. You need the insight I can give you that will strike at the heart of the problem. It is for this reason that I have given the Holy Spirit to be your Counsellor.

Jesus makes it clear that you will not be heard just because you use many words when you pray. Some of my children go on and on and on! **It is the few words I give them to pray by my Spirit that will prove effective, because He always knows what needs to be prayed in precise conformity with my will.** Sadly, people will not always accept you or what you say in my name. Some want to spend many hours being counselled rather than choosing to believe what I have already done for them.

Those who accept you accept me; and those who reject you reject me, because it was I who sent you. Does this rejection mean that you have failed to fulfil my purpose? Not at all. In my love and patience I need to speak to some people again and again before they will yield to me and submit to the truth of what I have spoken through various witnesses. So never be discouraged! You may be one whose words are rejected, but you have played a part in my overall purposes in that person's life. Pray that the time will come speedily when they will respond to the truth and be set free.

And remember, beloved, that you are in Jesus and He is in you. During His humanity, I lived in Him and did my work through Him. In your humanity it is I living in you by my Spirit who am doing my work in and through you. Your part is to trust me, to be in the place of agreement in faith and obedience so that I can work through you as I intend.

And remember what I have promised. If you love me and live in that agreement of obedience, both I and Jesus make our home with you. You see, beloved, we are at home where any of our children are in agreement with us.

Jude 20   Acts 3:16   Mark 13:13

60

My Rescue Mission

I am the way and the truth and the life.
No one comes to the Father except through me.
John 14:6

My beloved, you know me as your Father because I have chosen to reveal myself to you. Doesn't that make you feel honoured? Nobody can work their way into a relationship with me by meditating on their inner self, or any other such deception. I sent my Son to reveal my nature and character so that you may have a true revelation of who I am, to make it possible for you to know me as the Holy and Righteous One who loves you, chooses you and has a divine purpose for your life.

Beloved child, one of the things I expect of you is that you will be a faithful witness of the truth, that you will show others the way to know me so they too might receive my life.

People don't come to know me through debate and argument, exercises of the mind. It is true that you must be ready to explain your faith to others to give them understanding. However, someone is only born again and brought into a living relationship with me when they recognize their need of a change of heart, so don't aim at the intellect but at the heart when you want to communicate the gospel to others. Everyone has need. Often people will hide their needs behind intellectual debate, claiming they have no need of me while inwardly they are spiritually empty and are desperate for help.

Understand then, beloved, that you have accomplished nothing by winning an argument about religion when the heart need has not been addressed or touched. The flesh loves to discuss; the Spirit gives answers.

The woman at the well wanted to engage Jesus in argument about the right place to worship; Jesus changed the course of conversation to address her need. As a result she was changed so dramatically that her entire village came out to meet with Him, not to debate in philosophical discussion about the nature of God, but to know how such a transformation of life could take place.

The truth that no one comes to know me as Father except by Jesus greatly annoys those who are deceived, and you cannot engage in intellectual debate with deception. So aim for the heart. Uncover the needs in people's lives and show that I am the only one who can meet those needs: to be loved, accepted, set free, healed and filled with the life and power of God. Often the demonstration of my power will speak more to those of other religions than any amount of discussion and debate.

Be thankful, therefore, that you have received my life, and seek to make that life known to others. You don't want those who are deceived to join the deceiver in hell. Neither do you want people to come to the end of their lives here on earth without discovering why I gave them life in the first place. The thought of people coming for judgment without the protecting power of my blood is terrible!

This is why I sent Jesus to earth on a rescue mission: to rescue people from the devil, from themselves and their own folly. **Now I have made you part of this mission, to rescue people from darkness and lead them into the light so they too will become my disciples.** Then they too will rescue others and my Kingdom will advance on earth.

John 4:4–30   John 10:10   John 16:13–15

61

The Spirit of Faith

With that same spirit of faith we also believe and therefore speak.
2 Corinthians 4:13

My beloved child, I want to see all the dynamics of my Spirit working in your life because you need them all. Otherwise I would not have supplied them!

My Spirit is the Spirit of faith. He is the Spirit of love, of wisdom, of knowledge and understanding. He is the Spirit of truth. He is the Spirit of power and of the fear of the Lord.

Of course, if you allow things that grieve my Spirit to be expressed in your life, you will not see the outworking of my life and power in the way that is possible. Those things of the flesh, of self, always oppose the working of my Spirit and restrict the effectiveness of my Spirit within you.

Jesus manifested my life perfectly because there was nothing in Him that grieved me. He always obeyed the leading of the Spirit and would allow nothing to disrupt His unity with me.

I want *all* the dynamics of my Spirit to operate in your life. I don't want you to think you can choose some but neglect others, or to choose only what you consider the most necessary. I have made them all available to you, so you can appropriate them all and live in the good of them.

The Holy Spirit is the Spirit of faith. Many of my children struggle in the area of faith, especially when confronted with challenges. You need never say that you don't have enough faith, or that you are unable to believe, if I have placed the Spirit of faith within you. **In my grace I supply all the resources of faith you need through my Spirit.**

Paul says: 'With the same spirit of faith we believe and therefore speak.' The problem, beloved, is this. Some of my children don't allow the Spirit of faith to operate in their lives. They speak from the flesh, from their own perception, from a natural stand-point. Such natural and often negative speech undermines faith and disregards my words of promise. They speak about their problems from a worldly point of view, instead of seeing what I have done through Jesus to meet their need, and acknowledging that I am willing to give them my love and power through my grace. They don't appreciate that even in ordinary conversation their words are an expression of what is in their hearts, of what they actually believe.

Negative attitudes and unbelief are always in opposition to the work of my Spirit within you. If you have spent your time thinking and speaking about your problems, it is difficult to change suddenly from unbelief to faith because it is time to pray! This is like walking in the flesh all day long, and then trying to be spiritual when you pray.

You can see, beloved, if you live by faith there needs to be a consistency between what you say when you pray and when you speak at other times. **From the overflow of the heart the mouth speaks, no matter to whom you are speaking, or when!**

To live in my Spirit, to walk in agreement, is a walk of faith. I don't want you to walk in the flesh, depending on your own resources, speaking negative unbelief over your life as if you don't expect me to be gracious in meeting your need.

It grieves me to hear my children speaking continually about their sicknesses, problems and adversity, when all the time the resources of my grace are available to them and I have already met their needs on the cross.

I am not asking you to produce an unreal faith language, a series of slogans and clichés that sound good but don't come from your heart. No, the Spirit speaks the word of faith to your heart, the right word to believe in that particular situation. Listen to what He says, and speak and pray accordingly.

Submit yourself to the Spirit of faith at the beginning of every day, and pray that you will live and walk in that Spirit of faith, that with that same Spirit of faith you will believe

and therefore speak what I say about your circumstances. Yes, with that Spirit of faith you can see things as I see them, believe what I believe, speak over the situations as I myself would!

When I brought creation into being I simply spoke with that Spirit of faith. And look what happened as a result! When Jesus walked on earth, He spoke with that same Spirit of faith; and look what happened! With a few words the sick were healed, demons were cast out, the dead were raised, the storm was stilled, miracles were performed.

When Jesus heard of Lazarus' fatal illness, every word He spoke expressed His positive faith:

'This sickness will not end in death.'

'Lazarus has fallen asleep, but I am going there to wake him up.'

'Your brother will rise again.'

'I am the resurrection and the life. He who lives and believes in me will never die. Do you believe this?'

'Take away the stone.'

'Did I not tell you that if you believed, you would see the glory of God?'

Then Jesus looked up and said, 'Father, I thank you that you have heard me. I know that you always hear me, but I said this for the benefit of the people standing here, that they may believe you sent me.'

Jesus called in a loud voice, 'Lazarus, come out!'

With that same Spirit of faith, you can believe and therefore speak!

1 Corinthians 12:9   Proverbs 4:20–24   Luke 6:45

The Spirit of Wisdom

We speak of God's secret wisdom, a wisdom that has been hidden and that God destined for our glory before time began.
1 Corinthians 2:7

Beloved child, the Spirit of wisdom makes all the riches and resources of my wisdom available to you.

Jesus lived a life full of a wisdom very different from the wisdom of the world. People imagine that to collect information and knowledge makes them wise. This is deception. It makes them knowledgeable, but not wise. There are many knowledgeable people who sin and oppose my purposes. In my eyes sin is foolishness, the very opposite of wisdom.

The wisdom that comes from heaven, and that I impart, is first and foremost pure. This means that it shuns sin: it does not embrace it. It is wise to obey my word, to walk in holiness and righteousness. It is wise to seek first my Kingdom. You don't need a lot of worldly knowledge to do this! The gospel is the same for the most simple of people and for the most intellectual. All will be judged by me, not for their knowledge or intellectual prowess, but for their faith in Jesus and obedience to my will.

Those who allow my Spirit of wisdom to influence their lives embrace the holiness I desire to see in all my children.

My wisdom is peace-loving. Knowledge doesn't make you perfect! Many knowledgeable people try to obtain their objectives through violence, which I hate. It is wise to live at one with me, allowing me to use you to spread the gospel of peace and reconciliation.

My wisdom is considerate. Knowledge puffs up and makes people proud and selfish. Sin is selfish, placing self before others. Those who exhibit my wisdom put others before self; they are ready to work to alleviate their needs in any way they can. Love is neither rude nor self-seeking, and I am both Wisdom and Love.

Those motivated by my wisdom are submissive. They don't seek recognition for themselves or aim to be highly esteemed by others for either their knowledge or their actions. They know I pull down the proud but raise up the humble. They are not wise in their own eyes, but have a sober estimate of themselves. They humble themselves before my word, preferring to believe what I say rather than their own opinions and ideas.

Wisdom encourages you to submit even your intellect to me, so that you may allow the mind of Christ to influence your natural mind. Remember, you have the mind of Christ in your spirit, but your natural mind in your soul. It is wise to submit your soul to your spirit; then you will understand how I think about you and the circumstances that face you.

My wisdom is full of mercy and compassion towards others. It is the merciful who obtain mercy; therefore it is always wise to be merciful and compassionate towards others. The flesh always desires the very opposite of wisdom! Those who walk in the flesh judge and criticize others rather than expressing mercy towards them.

Where can knowledge lead someone eternally? Will a person's knowledge of worldly things help them to attain the riches of heaven? Even theological knowledge will not help them if they do not come before me with clean hands and a pure heart!

My wisdom causes you to be fruitful. This is what gives me glory, that you bear much fruit and so prove to be my disciples. To walk in the way of my wisdom is to follow the leading of my Spirit, who will effect this fruitfulness. You will never be fruitful or effective by listening to your own 'wisdom' or understanding! The Spirit of wisdom tells you not only what to do but the most effective way of doing it.

My wisdom is impartial. Those motivated by worldly wisdom see things only through their own limited understanding. They fight for parties and causes, rather than my Kingdom. I don't take sides in disputes; often there is partial truth on both sides. The real question is: 'Who is on *my* side?' Those who are seeking first the Kingdom of God and my righteousness.

And my wisdom is sincere. It seeks the welfare of my Kingdom, and therefore of my people. It is concerned about fulfilling *my* purposes, whereas those who put their confidence in their own understanding have their own agendas.

Are you not blessed, beloved, to possess my Spirit of wisdom? Is it not best, therefore, that you seek to live in that wisdom? To do so will surely please me!

James 3:17   1 Corinthians 2:6–8   Matthew 5:7

63

The Spirit of Revelation

We have not received the spirit of the world but the Spirit who is from God, that we may understand what God has freely given us.
1 Corinthians 2:12

My beloved, you not only have the Spirit of wisdom but also the Spirit of revelation. Did Jesus not promise that my Spirit of truth would guide you into all the truth, that He would take my words and reveal them to you? The Spirit of revelation brings my word to life in you, so that my word becomes my voice to you personally.

The more you understand my ways, the more readily you will walk in them. There is a difference between spiritual knowledge and understanding. You can be knowledgeable about spiritual things, but **the person of understanding knows how important it is to live by what they hear, to apply that knowledge to the practical circumstances of their life, so that they live in the good of what they know.**

It is the Spirit of revelation that gives this understanding but also causes my word to become prophetic, making it the 'now' word appropriate for the immediate situation. Obedience to the word of revelation enables you to walk in victory, for my Spirit will always give you the right word at the right time, the word that will prove effective in your situation when you act upon it.

It is exciting, beloved, when my Spirit speaks to your heart. Never tire of that excitement. Expect such inspiration whenever you read my word, that my Spirit will not only speak personally and directly to you but will also increase your understanding. This is not natural understanding, but spiritual understanding that can come only from my Spirit, revelation to understand the extent of my grace, of all that I have freely given you in Christ. Believe that you have in Christ what I say you have, so that you don't ask me to give what I have already given!

Be thankful that I have given you the Spirit of faith, the Spirit of love, the Spirit of wisdom and the Spirit of revelation, of understanding. Each of these dynamics of my Holy Spirit can operate fully in your life. Yes, my beloved child, you can live in the good of what you know you possess through my grace. Ignorance and unbelief will rob you of the ability to live in these riches.

These different aspects of the working of my Holy Spirit combine together to be a powerful presence in your life. Rejoice in the goodness of my grace! Welcome every opportunity to receive further revelation of all I have graciously given you in my beloved Son.

John 14:26   John 10:3–8   Isaiah 11:2

64

The Power of the Spirit

But you will receive power when the Holy Spirit comes on you.
Acts 1:8

When I filled you with my Spirit, my beloved, you received my power. I am able to do much more than you can ask or imagine, according to that power at work within you, a power so great that it more than compensates for your weakness. My grace is sufficient for you, and my power is made perfect in your weakness.

Can you see why the enemy tries to get you to concentrate on your weakness? He suggests you are so weak that you will fail; you don't have the power to succeed. He is a liar. Your weakness is the very secret of my power. Paul knew this and said: 'When I am weak, then I am strong.'

He prayed that out of my glorious riches my children would be strengthened with my power, through my Spirit at work in their inner beings. Beloved child, this is a prayer from my heart; it is what I want for you. You really cannot imagine the great things I can do in you and through you by my Spirit!

This power enables you to do whatever I ask of you, to fulfil my purpose for you. Beloved child, you can trust in yourself and in your own weakness – in which case you will inevitably fail again and again. Or, in your weakness, you can trust in the power of my Spirit, in which case He will enable you again and again so that you will not fail.

The enemy cannot take away what I have given you. He can only try to undermine your confidence, so that instead of trusting in my power you strive in your own strength. He is not afraid of your power, but he has no answer to *mine*! He that is in you is greater than he that is in the world. **When you confront the enemy with my power he is defeated**. You can inflict defeat on him in one situation after another.

To follow the leading of my Spirit will certainly curb the influence of your flesh-life, but will also release more of my power in your life. **This power enables you to be a faithful witness. It enables you to resist temptation and to overcome the attacks of the enemy, and to do whatever I ask of you.**

Rivers of this power can also flow out of your life to others around you; in my name you can heal and see people set free. For this power is the same power that was at work in Jesus' own ministry. **It is the power of His Spirit, the power that enables you to do the same things as He has done.**

Can you not see, beloved, that if it is my power which does these things effectively, it doesn't matter what channel of my grace I choose to use? Yes, I can use *you*; that power can flow through you. The power is not in the channel itself, but in the life that flows through the channel.

However, as with Jesus, the exercise of that power is coupled with authority. He was recognized even by His opponents as a man of authority. The demons knew the source of that supernatural authority before even His disciples understood.

I have not only given you power by my Spirit, but I have given you authority to pray, to speak and act in my name. I have given you authority over all the works of the devil. I have given you authority to prevent on earth what is not allowed in heaven; and release on earth what is released from heaven.

I am teaching you to exercise authority so that you can see more evidence of my power in your life. **This involves first submitting yourself to my authority; you can exercise my authority effectively only by living under my authority.** When you do so, you release whatever power is necessary to enable you to overcome.

The deceiver wants you to doubt the authority you have so that you don't exercise the power you have over him. He has no answer to the authority of Christ in you.

Beloved, you have the authority I tell you that you have. So you can do what I say you can do! I love to see you exercise that authority, to see the devil fleeing from you. I love to see you overcome because you are exercising the authority and power I have given you.

1 Corinthians 2:4–5   1 Thessalonians 1:4–5   Luke 10:19–20

65

The Fear of the Lord

He will delight in the fear of the LORD.
Isaiah 11:3

Surely his salvation is near those who fear him,
that his glory may dwell in our land.
Psalm 85:9

My beloved, it may seem strange to you that Jesus delighted in the fear of the Lord. What effect did this have on His life and ministry? He never grieved me. He always lived in obedience to my will and lived a life of perfect submission to me. He hated wickedness; He had no desire to sin or grieve me but loved righteousness instead.

Beloved child, I want you to be like Him! **I want the Spirit of the fear of the Lord to be a powerful force in your life.** This means that you will not want to offend me, grieve me or disobey me.

I have not given you a spirit of fear, of being afraid in a negative sense; I have given you a spirit of love, power and a sound mind. The only fear I want in you is the same as the only fear that was in Jesus: a holy fear, the Spirit of the fear of the Lord.

Do you want my Holy Spirit to impact your life in this way? Unless you do, you will continue to struggle against sin. You will know what you ought to do without having the right motivation to do it! You will set your will against mine, choosing to please me sometimes, but choosing to please self at other times. You will say that you want to be obedient without actually being obedient.

It is the Spirit of the fear of the Lord that enables you to live the life of holiness to which I call every one of my children, that will enable every yoke of sin to be broken.

Those who fear me have a proper reverence towards me and my purposes. My Church can only impact the nations when my own children live in the fear of their God. **How will those living in darkness be brought to submission unless those I call to live and share the good news with others are themselves living in reverence for me, for my word, for my Spirit, for my will and my ways?**

Yes, beloved, whenever there is proper reverence for me in the Church then the world is impacted by the gospel of truth. This is why in times of genuine revival you see the Spirit of the fear of the Lord operating among my people. They are then convicted readily of their sinful state and turn to me with repentance and faith. They live in the fear of God, so radical is the transformation that takes place in their lives.

When my people fear me, my glory is in the land. And that is what you want, isn't it, beloved? To see my glory in your land, a harvest of souls coming out of darkness into the glorious light of my Kingdom!

Psalm 85:9   Revelation 14:6–7   Psalm 34:9

66

The Agreement of Faith

If anyone chooses to do God's will, he will find out whether my teaching comes from God or whether I speak on my own.
John 7:17

My beloved, you believe that Jesus is my Son; so His words come to you with my divine authority. They are the words I gave Him to speak.

I call you to live in fellowship with me, to abide in me, to share in my life; for my words to abide or live in you. My words can only live in you if you agree with what I say! Then you can ask for whatever you wish and I will give it to you.

Does this promise conflict with your previous experience? Well, let me ask you if you have fulfilled the conditional statement. Have you lived in agreement with Jesus, and have His words lived in you?

While you judge and even reject some of what He says, then clearly His words don't live in you in the way He intends. Did He not teach that you will receive whatever you ask for in prayer if you believe? You not only need to agree with Him about what it is right to pray, but you need also to agree with what the outcome will be!

When praying with faith, you are not in any doubt about what answer you will receive. If you pray truly in the name of Jesus, you agree with His expectations as to the outcome of your prayer.

He also taught that whatever you ask in prayer, you are to believe you *have* received and it will be yours! How can you believe you have received at the time you pray unless you are sure about the outcome?

Faith is being sure of what you hope for and certain of what you do not see. Put in its simplest terms, faith is being sure and certain. The one praying with faith is not double-minded about the outcome of the prayer. Those who are double-minded are unstable in all their ways and cannot expect to receive anything from me!

When in agreement with me you are not unstable: you are on the Rock! The one who is in agreement with me will not be double-minded. I am certainly not double-minded; I am always sure and certain about what I shall do.

Neither was Jesus ever double-minded, which is why He taught the people to be sure and certain when they prayed. He told them to ask and they would receive. He even said that all who asked would receive. Seek and you will find. Knock and it will be opened to you. There is no reason to accept any other answer than the one prayed for!

Can you see, therefore, the need to walk in agreement with me? Answered prayer is the fruit of such a walk and gives me glory. Is this impossible for you? Not at all! You have my word and my Spirit. I have equipped you fully for just such a life of faith. However, the choice is yours. You have to agree with me, not me with you!

I want you to live in such agreement. Then you will exhibit the kind of faith of which Jesus spoke, the faith to see mountains of need removed.

Because faith places you in agreement with me and I am so great, you need faith the size of a tiny seed to see miracles happen. When planted, a seed germinates and bears fruit; it is faith that expects results. All you have to do is sow the seed, not produce the result; that is my job! You see how powerful the prayer of faith is.

If you live in disagreement with me, it is not easy to come suddenly into agreement because you are confronted with a particular need. I want you to live in agreement with me so that, when need arises, you are already in a position of faith to be able to respond positively and victoriously to the situation.

Hebrews 12:1   James 1:8   Matthew 18:19–20

67

Pray in Agreement with Me

*I tell you the truth, my Father will give you whatever you ask
in my name. Until now you have not asked for anything in my
name. Ask and you will receive, and your joy will be complete.*
John 16:23–24

Agree with me, my beloved! Jesus made this promise to His
disciples when speaking to them about sending them the gift of
the Holy Spirit, who would enable them to act and speak in His
name. They could only do in the name of Jesus what His Spirit
told them to do. They could only speak in His name the words
He gave them to speak.

The same principle is true about praying in His name. To pray
in His name is to pray what Jesus would pray, and believe what
He is telling you to believe will be the outcome of that prayer.

I always honour my Son because of the way in which He lived
His life in perfect obedience to me. I honour the shedding of His
blood by forgiving those who confess their sins to me. Because I
honour Jesus, I honour those who walk with Him, those who
live in Him and in whom His words live. I honoured Jesus by
always answering His prayer. **When you pray truly in His
name, you are praying in agreement with Him; and so I shall
do whatever you ask. I will honour your prayer.** Again,
beloved, this is fruit produced from agreeing with Jesus.

But what if one of my children has not been living in agreement
with Jesus and a need arises in their life? Will I be deaf to the
prayer of my child? Not at all! But that child needs to repent as
well as believe, to have a change of heart and mind, to come into
agreement with Jesus, not just about that issue but concerning
anything in his or her life that is in disagreement with me.

If two walk together they are agreed. **I want my child to come
back to a walk of agreement, not just a prayer of agreement.**

However, in my love, mercy and grace I don't delay the answer to the prayer until I see the evidence of such a walk. I don't ask you to earn the answers to your needs by your own works, only to do my work – which is to believe in Jesus. I am the God of grace.

I read the hearts of my children. I can see whether they agree with Jesus or not. Without such agreement, they may use the name of Jesus but they are not truly praying in His name. I cannot be deceived; I can see only too well what each truly believes will be the outcome of their prayer.

Understand this, my beloved: I always want to give to my children. Every claim you can make on my love and grace is through Jesus Christ your Lord. Every prayer comes to me through Him, therefore: through agreement with Him, through faith in Him.

So it is true: you will receive whatever you ask in prayer if you believe, if there is that agreement of faith. If you believe what I believe. If you expect what I expect. Truly, I will give you whatever you ask in the name of Jesus!

Beloved, you may feel like those first disciples as I explain these things to you, that until now you have not asked for anything in the name of Jesus in the true sense. Don't dwell on the past. You prayed then according to the revelation you had at that time. There have been times when, although you thought you were praying with faith, you were double-minded about the outcome.

I know also there have been occasions when you thought you were sure and certain; this was not because you were in agreement with Jesus, but because you were listening to your own soul, to your emotions, not to the voice of my Spirit. How can you tell the difference between listening to the soul and to my Spirit? When you listen to your own feelings you are convinced I am going to do something: I will heal, I will provide, I will be gracious. What you say is in the future. Jesus explains that faith knows I have healed, I have provided, I have answered, even though there may be no visible evidence of this. This is why He said that, whatever you ask, you are to believe you *have* received

165

– not you *will* receive. When you believe you have received it, then it will be yours, He promises.

You *can* walk in agreement with Jesus because His blood has already put you into that position. You *can* abide in Him and let His words abide in you. You *can* pray in the name of Jesus and see the fulfilment of what He has promised.

If you are in agreement with Jesus, you are not going to ask for anything in the flesh, but only what pleases the Spirit. You will not pray for anything that opposes His will. And if you are in agreement with Him you will ask with the utmost confidence, knowing that you have received whatever you ask in His name.

My servant John heard Jesus give these promises about answered prayer. He walked with Jesus in the Spirit for about fifty years, and then wrote: 'If our hearts do not condemn us, we have confidence before God and receive from Him whatever we ask because we obey His commands and do what pleases Him.'

Do you understand, beloved? He was speaking of the fruit of a life lived in agreement with Jesus. For if you live in agreement with Him, your heart will not condemn you; you will have confidence before me. To walk in agreement with Him will mean that you seek to obey His word and do what pleases Him.

You can live and pray in agreement with Him.

John 14:13–14   John 15:16   Luke 11:9–10

68

Listen to My Words

My son, pay attention to what I say; listen closely to my words.
Do not let them out of your sight, keep them within your heart;
for they are life to those who find them and health to a
man's whole body.
Proverbs 4:20–22

My beloved, I speak to you as your Father, who loves you and cares for you. So I want you to pay close attention to what I say. Every time I speak to you, through my word or by my Spirit, it is always with purpose. I speak words of direction, of forgiveness, of release and healing to you. Every time you believe what I say you receive something positive; the truth sets you free.

Yes, there are times I need to speak words of warning, of correction and even of discipline for your own good, a demonstration of my love for you. For a loving father disciplines his child when necessary. However, I am never hard-hearted or legalistic in my attitudes, although I will not compromise my standards for you or for anyone! I will not change my word to accommodate your wishes, neither will I reduce what I say to the level of your faith. Rather, I want to lift your faith to the level of my word.

You see, beloved, my words bring life and health to those who believe. Those who substitute their own ideas for what I say cannot receive that life or health from their own opinions!

Always remember that, because I created humanity, I understand how people function and how their bodies work physically. Jesus healed people of a variety of conditions, physical, emotional and spiritual.

Notice how often people were healed by believing what He said. Those words He spoke then have the same life and power today, when people believe in the same way now as they did then. When such faith exists today, that same life and power touches people's lives and sets them free.

I urge you to pay close attention to my words and not let them out of your sight. I want you to receive the spirit and life they contain. I want you to continue in my word, be my disciple and know that the truth sets you free.

I want the words in my book to live in your heart. My Spirit is like the sower who sows those seeds into your heart, that they may bear much fruit.

I don't want your heart to be hard, like the path that could not receive the word. Neither do I want your faith to be shallow, so that you believe when you first hear what I say but soon become distracted by the circumstances, losing sight of my words so they cannot be deeply rooted in your heart. When a person's faith in my word is shallow, they feel unable to cope in times of pressure. They believe their feelings rather than persevering in the truth.

I don't want you to allow anything to grow in your life that will stifle the good seed of my word. Negative thoughts and attitudes contradict the truth of my word, together with such things as worry and putting your trust in your worldly assets instead of in my Father love for you. Pull up those weeds – anything not in agreement with what I say.

The one who bears much fruit holds on to my word with an honest and good heart! That is the kind of heart you are to have, my beloved: a believing heart that wants to obey my word as your expression of true love for me. You will reproduce thirty, sixty, a hundred times what was sown!

Hebrews 12:5–6   Matthew 13:18–23   Proverbs 3:1–2

69

Sow My Words

*He was pierced for our transgressions, he was crushed for
our iniquities; the punishment that brought us peace was upon
him, and by his wounds we are healed.*
Isaiah 53:5

My beloved, because I have loved you, I have provided for all
that is necessary for your forgiveness and healing – of spirit, soul
and body. What Jesus did for you on the cross is a complete and
perfect work covering every need you could have. Your inheritance is made possible through His sacrifice. And your healing is
part of that inheritance.

Some of my beloved ones don't appreciate this. They approach
the whole subject of healing as if I am double-minded about the
issue, deciding to heal some but not others. They come to this
conclusion because they see that some receive miracles of my
healing grace, but not others.

Listen carefully: all that I have is yours. It is yours already,
including your healing. I have provided it as part of your inheritance. There is nothing double-minded about that!

Do you feel unworthy to receive a miracle? It is only guilt that
makes you unworthy, and Jesus took all your sins upon Himself
so your guilt could be taken away! His forgiveness removes your
unworthiness so that you are able to receive my healing grace.

This is not a matter of argument or debate, but of simple faith
in what He has done and made available to you through the love
He displayed on the cross.

Whenever you look at the circumstances, at the symptoms,
the pain, the need, it is difficult to believe this. This is like
looking at the mountain instead of commanding it to be moved!
Many of my children keep describing the mountain to others
instead of speaking to it with faith and authority. Of course, a

person who doesn't agree with what I say cannot speak with authority or pray in the name of Jesus. How can people pray with faith if they don't believe I want to heal them? I would hardly have made provision for your healing if I was unsure whether I wanted to heal or not!

Some are afraid to ask in case they don't receive! That is the measure of their unbelief.

What of those with chronic needs? Does it make any difference to the outcome of faith if the need is great? For me, it is no more difficult to raise the dead than to heal a cold. But for you it is more difficult to believe, until you understand the principle of sowing and reaping.

I watch over my word to perform it. Jesus makes it clear that the word is like seed. Although the seed in your hand is good, it cannot be fruitful until planted. You can have a barn full of seed, but it will still produce nothing until planted. You have a Bible full of the finest spiritual seeds, but until those words are planted they cannot produce the life of which they speak.

When the Holy Spirit speaks to your heart, you need to take what He says and sow it. When you read or hear my word and faith rises in your heart, sow that word with faith.

Understand, though, that all the words you speak are seeds. When you speak negatively of yourself, of others or your circumstances, you sow negative seeds. Each seed produces after its own kind; wheat seeds can only produce wheat, and negative seeds produce negative results. On the other hand, seeds of healing produce healing when planted with faith.

When you speak of sickness, you sow seeds of sickness that will produce a harvest of sickness. When you sow seeds of healing, they produce a harvest of healing. This is why I say that my words are life and health to a person's whole body!

Seeds are very powerful; once sown, they can even push through paving. Yet in the hand they will produce nothing, no matter how good the quality of the seed!

And so, beloved one, I want you to sow the good seed of my word in prayer and water it with faith and thanksgiving! It will produce after its own kind. The seed cannot produce any other kind of life than that which is contained in the seed. Seeds of healing, sown in faith, will reap a harvest of healing; they cannot produce anything else!

When farmers sow the seed, they believe they will see the harvest. They know that some seed bears fruit more rapidly than other seed, and they have to await the growth period. During that time they don't dig up the seed to ensure it is germinating. No, they eagerly await the signs which prove that what they have sown is springing up with life. They expect to see the shoot breaking the surface and then beginning to grow.

I want you to sow good seed and to be looking expectantly for the evidence that the seed is bearing after its own kind.

How do you sow? Pray according to my word. Speak words of truth over your life. See yourself as I see you: made whole in my Son, Jesus. And be thankful for my healing grace at work within you.

Matthew 8:2–3   Matthew 8:8–10   Matthew 8:16–17

It Is Finished

It is finished.
John 19:30

Yes, my beloved, there was a great cry of triumph from the cross: 'It is finished. It is done. It is completed.'

Do you realize why Jesus said this? He had taken upon Himself all your sin, sickness, pain, grief and sorrow. He was punished and even crushed for your sake. The total work of salvation needed had been accomplished. Every human condition and need had been met.

He had fulfilled His call as the Lamb of God, the sacrifice I myself had provided to take away the sins of the world. It was a painful end to His human ministry, but He knew this death would be followed by resurrection and a return to the glory He had with me before creation began. The cost was far outweighed by the glory that was set before Him.

Jesus' cry from the cross was a cry of triumph for you. Everything needed for your healing and salvation of spirit, soul and body was accomplished. You can echo this cry: 'It is done. It is finished. It is completed. It is accomplished.' You are now free because of all that Jesus did for you!

If you believe this, you will rejoice and be glad in the fact that He has done everything needed for your complete forgiveness, healing and restoration to a life of unity with me. He has brought you into agreement with me. So agree with what I say: 'It is finished!' It is done: be thankful. Remember that in this sacrificial act, I declared my love for you. The cross, and all that Jesus suffered and accomplished, shows how much I love you, a love that can never be withdrawn.

Listen, my beloved: I don't condemn any who fail to take hold of the full riches made available through their salvation, and I don't want you to condemn them either! I work within their hearts to inspire faith. I raise up men and women of faith to encourage them. You cannot blame me if some choose to reject what I say.

You hear of wonderful miracles of my grace when people are raised from their death-bed or rise out of their wheelchairs and walk. You hear of cancers disappearing, blind eyes being opened and even deformities being healed. Yes, you hear of these things happening today.

You long to see more of these things for yourself, thankful that every person so healed has received a wonderful work of my grace. But you are also mystified. If such things happen in some places, why don't they happen everywhere? If they take place on some occasions, why don't they occur all the time? Does it require an immense amount of faith, greater than most could ever acquire? Do such things happen only where there is no medical help to fall back on?

I answer the prayers of my children. Some regard me as their only course of action and throw themselves on my mercy.

I delight to respond to their cries. Yes, my beloved, sometimes there is a note of desperation and determination about faith, as was evident in many of those who were healed by Jesus in the gospels. I respond to such faith that believes that no matter how dire the situation appears to be, one word from me or a touch of my divine hand will immediately change the circumstances.

Those who came to Jesus not only believed that He could heal them, but that He would. He would speak the necessary word, or perform the right action and they, or those on whose behalf they came, would be healed. This is why Jesus said: 'Your faith has made you well' and 'As you believe, so let it be.'

Beloved child, you have faith. Choose to believe me, not the circumstances. Sow words of truth and expect to see the harvest of my grace. Remember, having sown the word with faith, keep watering it with thanksgiving.

Revelation 7:9–10   Revelation 5:8–10   Matthew 8:13

71

The Testing of Your Faith

You may have had to suffer grief in all kinds of trials. These have come so that your faith – of greater worth than gold, which perishes even though refined by fire – may be proved genuine and may result in praise, glory and honour when Jesus Christ is revealed.
1 Peter 1:6–7

Beloved, those who overcome will inherit the crown of life! In order to be an overcomer, you have to have situations to overcome. It should not surprise you, therefore, that there will be times when your faith in me will be tested.

Your faith has to be proved. It cannot be theoretical, for faith without works is dead. I want you to see, and I want others to witness, that even when you have to face adversity you overcome because you maintain your trust in me. I want you to demonstrate that you are not fighting in your strength to get the victory, but that you trust in the One who has already overcome on your behalf.

You see, beloved, your faith in me is more precious than gold. But just as gold has to be refined by fire, so your faith is refined by the testing situations that confront you. These trials must never cause you to question my love for you. Jesus makes it clear that in the world you will experience trials and tribulation. Keep the shield of faith in one hand, and the sword of the Spirit that is the word of God in the other hand, at all times. The shield of faith is able to quench *all* the fiery darts the enemy fires at you. If your shield of faith is in place, none of those arrows will wound you. There is no point in allowing the enemy to inflict wounds on you and then putting the shield of faith in place. It is too late by then! Better to have your defences intact before the attack comes. You don't have to receive any of the lies and temptations he directs at you. Neither do you need to accept sickness as my will for you.

The shield of faith is your defence weapon. However, you are able to move on the attack by wielding the sword of the Spirit, the word of God. My children overcome the enemy by the Blood of the Lamb and the word of their testimony. That word of your testimony is your faith in all Jesus has accomplished for you; your trust is in His completed work. I have already defeated the enemy by the shedding of my blood, overcoming sin, sickness and every demonic power. So you stand strong in *my* victory. This is the word to speak over your life: that the enemy is overcome and defeated. **Your faith is in the victory I have won, not in your own ability to fight.**

Listen, beloved: when you are wounded, I don't condemn you. I want to heal and restore you! When you sin I don't throw you out of my Kingdom. I am ready to forgive and restore you to righteousness. Undergoing trials can cause grief; but Jesus took your grief upon Himself when He went to the cross so that you don't need to be overcome by it.

Have you received the message? You don't need to be overcome by sin, sickness, suffering or adversity of any kind. My grace will enable you to overcome! And your faith will be proved genuine.

James 1:2–4   Ephesians 6:10–18   1 John 5:4

72

I Am Your Holy Father

Hallowed be your name.
Luke 11:2

My beloved, I am your *holy* Father. You are loved and accepted by the One who is holy. I couldn't accept you if you were unholy; you couldn't be one with me unless you had been made holy in my sight! How could such a thing have happened?

You are only too aware that you could do nothing to make yourself holy. In fact, you had no desire to be holy, did you? So how could it be that now I regard you not only as my beloved, a child of grace and destiny, but also as my holy child?

First, you need to understand that to be holy means that you have been set apart. Yes, beloved, you have been called and set apart for me, that I might love you and ensure that you fulfil the purpose which I have for you. I will remind you of some of the truths I have been teaching you so you can understand in what sense I regard you as holy.

You have been set apart from your old life of sin and disobedience. You have been set apart from the devil; you no longer serve him; he is no longer your father. You have been set apart from the world, so that you don't have to conform any longer to the world's way of thinking. Instead, you belong to me and can live the life of my Kingdom here on earth.

So you are set apart for me, to love me, serve me and honour me by seeking first my Kingdom and my righteousness in your life.

Your life, then, is consecrated to my purposes; this is why I paid the price for you. You don't belong to yourself; you belong to me. It is I who have purchased you for myself, for my Kingdom to come and my will to be done in your life! **You are holy because you belong to the Holy One. This is not**

something that ought to be true; it already is true. You do not have to strive to become holy; you already are holy!

Is this a frightening thought? What of the unholy things of which you are so conscious, those thoughts, words and actions that are certainly not holy in my sight? Surely these things are evidences of unholiness, not holiness? Don't those things disqualify you from any idea of already being holy? No, because of my great mercy and grace!

Remember, I have taken hold of your life and placed you in Christ. I don't see you apart from Him; I see you in Him. He came and identified totally with you in His human life so that now you can be totally identified with Him in His risen life.

You were not only crucified with Christ; you were raised to a new life with Him. It is not your holiness that makes you acceptable to me, but His holiness. You are righteous in my sight because you live in the Righteous One. His righteousness has become your righteousness!

This is the result of my great love for you and the grace I have shown you. I don't treat you as you deserve but as one who lives in my Son. So I always want to treat you as I treat Him; to give to you as I gave to Him when He lived on earth.

Is this remarkable? Yes, but it is true. **You are accepted by me in the Beloved, not through what you have done, but because of all He has done for you. You are holy, not because of what you have done, but because you are in Him. You are righteous, not because of what you have done, but because you live in the One who is Righteous.** Realize this, beloved one: His life is your life. All His riches and resources are yours; they are available to you as a gift of my grace. You don't deserve them, could never earn them, yet they are yours!

Should you not rejoice in these great truths? They only seem unreal to you because you don't believe I could love you so deeply. Yet I do. I have loved you with an everlasting love, my perfect love that will never fade or change. It is because of this great love that I have made you a co-heir with Christ and given you such a rich inheritance in heaven.

It is that same love that will enable you to fulfil your destiny in this life. Jesus fulfilled the mission on which I sent Him and now reigns in glory. It is my purpose that you fulfil the purpose to which I have called you; and that you, too, will reign with Him in glory!

So what of the unholy thoughts and actions that persist in your life? Such things are out of place, aren't they? It is not that you are unholy and should be holy; you are holy and don't need to act in an unholy way. In your old life you were unholy; as a new creation you are holy. I want you to see yourself as I see you, to agree with me about how I perceive your life. After all, if you disagree with me, someone has to be wrong; and it isn't me!

If you think of yourself as unholy, you will inevitably think, speak and act accordingly. However, if you see yourself as holy and realize that you can walk in holiness, then you will resist those things you know to be unholy and a contradiction to my will. My blood has made you holy, and restores you to holiness every time you are forgiven.

1 Corinthians 1:30   John 17:17   John 15:3

73

The Kingdom of Righteousness

For the kingdom of God is ... righteousness, peace and joy in the
Holy Spirit, because anyone who serves Christ in this way is
pleasing to God and approved by men.
Romans 14:17–18

My beloved, nothing is gained by condemning those in darkness. They need to be saved, not condemned. This is why Jesus said that, although all judgment had been entrusted to Him, He hadn't come to judge but to save.

Because you are a child of light, I want you to live the life of the Kingdom of God here on earth. You now know that this means living in agreement with me. Then you can influence those who are not in agreement with me.

Righteousness is the sceptre of my Kingdom, and the sceptre is the symbol of authority. And so, beloved, living in righteousness gives you authority over the darkness. It is the fervent prayers of the righteous that are powerful and effective!

If you live in agreement with me you live in righteousness, even if there is unrighteousness all around you in the world. Don't allow that unrighteousness to have any influence over you. Don't compromise the righteous standards by which I call you to live, otherwise you will move out of agreement with me into disagreement. You might find favour with the world, but only at the expense of grieving me!

When you grieve me you lose both your peace and your joy. That in turn affects your confidence and ability to exercise my authority.

To walk in righteousness will not only please me but will give you the approval and respect of men. Yes, many who live in unrighteousness respect believers who hold to their principles and refuse to compromise. You will also be a good example to other believers, and especially to young people. They need to see my sons and daughters living in integrity and truth, people unwilling to compromise with the world, either to feed their fleshly desires or for some financial gain.

The devil is the father of unrighteousness. So it pleases him when you or any of my children forsake my ways. Beloved, when you have the choice between righteousness and unrighteousness and you choose unrighteousness, you only have to ask yourself why you made that particular choice, and immediately you will be aware of your selfish motives.

You cannot see my Kingdom purposes without seeking to be righteous. And this will often involve denying your selfish motives, so that you can remain in agreement with me, faithful and obedient. My beloved child, the rewards for righteousness far outweigh any gains from unrighteousness. The rewards for righteousness are eternal; any gains for unrighteousness are only temporary and lead to bondage.

Because I am the righteous Lord I exercise particular care over my children who walk in righteousness. Because of the cleansing power of my blood, you have been cleansed from all unrighteousness; and my Holy Spirit living within you will enable you to live in righteousness, peace and joy. Better to please your Lord, who is Light, than walk in unrighteousness and please the prince of darkness!

You understand these things by now. I remind you of them because in your walk with me it is not what you know that matters, but what you do with what you know! Knowing the truth does not profit anyone unless he or she walks in the truth. Knowing you are holy and righteous before me is an encouragement to live a life pleasing me, thankful that I have chosen you and set you apart for myself. Yes, beloved, you were my choice!

Galatians 3:11   Ephesians 4:22–24   Philippians 1:9–11

74

Jesus' Strategy

*For he has rescued us from the dominion of darkness
and brought us into the kingdom of the Son he loves.*
Colossians 1:13

The crowds were attracted to Jesus because He lived in agreement with me. He revealed my heart of love and compassion. Do you realize, my beloved, that the more you live in agreement with me, the more you will reveal my love and compassion to others? Those in need will be drawn to you, for they will sense that you don't judge or condemn them for the problems they face, but that you accept them and want to help them.

I want to teach you something very important, my beloved, about the strategy by which I work. You see, there is much wrong in the society in which you live. There is much that is opposed to my will and purpose. You can deplore the increasing immorality and the falling standards in righteousness. You can deplore the corruption that exists, even among those who govern or have influence.

When Jesus was on earth, He was surrounded by similar problems. Yet He didn't come as a social reformer; He didn't lead protest campaigns, nor did He make public addresses deploring the state of the nation or judging the Roman occupying forces.

Obviously, there was much He could have said. What criticisms He made He reserved for the false and hypocritical religious leaders. Of course, He could have made more political statements and have had an agenda for social reform. But this was not His strategy.

He aimed at the hearts of men and women, rather than the issues, for He knew it was impossible to resolve issues without a change of heart. He came with the gift of my heavenly Kingdom. Those who embraced that Kingdom would be given new hearts and would have dramatic changes in their priorities; they were to be light to those still in darkness.

You see, beloved, Jesus didn't criticize the darkness for being darkness. No, He shone His light into the darkness and all who received that light were delivered from the darkness. They in turn could become instruments through whom more light could be shone into the darkness.

He came as light into the darkness, and even though the darkness didn't receive Him He still didn't condemn those who rejected Him, but forgave them. He even prayed for the forgiveness of those who were responsible for His crucifixion, because they didn't understand what they were doing.

The god of this age has blinded the minds of unbelievers so that they cannot see the light of the gospel of the glory of Christ. Don't judge or condemn them, beloved. Those who are blinded to the truth live in darkness, and so it is hardly surprising that they pursue the works of darkness!

Learn from Jesus' strategy. **Instead of condemning those in darkness, seek for ways to shine the light of my truth into this darkness. Be one of the labourers that I send out into the harvest.** And understand this: the deeper the darkness, the more people there are who are desperate to be delivered from that darkness. Most of them simply don't know where to turn in their desperation. Those who cry out to me, even in desperation, I save.

There is little point in arguing with those in darkness. They cannot understand what can only be seen in the light. Lead them to the light so that they can be delivered from all the effects of darkness and become children of light. Only then will they turn away from the deeds of darkness and embrace the standards of righteousness that belong to my Kingdom. Only then can they too live in agreement with me. You can be sure that any who turn to me in repentance and faith, I will take out of the dominion of darkness and place in my Kingdom!

Did Jesus have no interest in social problems or reform? He didn't come to reform but to make new. This is what made

His mission unique. And today you are part of that unique mission.

I want my Church, my Body here on earth, to manifest the life of my Kingdom. If people see the example of selfless love, the fruit of faith and the many advantages of being in agreement with me, then many will choose to turn from the darkness and will embrace the truth of my Kingdom and be set free. The darker things become in society around you, the more desperate people will become for the light. And you, beloved, are a child of light.

John 3:19–21   Matthew 5:16   Ephesians 3:20–21

75

Those Outside the Kingdom

Outside are the dogs, those who practice magic arts, the sexually immoral, the murderers, the idolaters and everyone who loves and practices falsehood.
Revelation 22:15

My beloved, Jesus shone His light into the darkness. He didn't judge those in darkness, but He did warn of the dangers of rejecting Him and remaining in the darkness. Their darkness would become eternal darkness.

I don't want you to frighten people into my Kingdom; I want to draw them by love. However, there will be occasions when you will need to warn people of the consequences of rejecting me, so you need to know what Jesus taught about this.

Because I loved the world I sent Jesus, so that whoever believes in Him shall not perish eternally but have eternal life. I didn't send Him to condemn the world, but that the world would be saved through Him. Remember, then, that it is never my desire to condemn.

However, Jesus warned that those who do not believe in Him stand condemned already, simply because they do not believe in the One I have sent to save them from the condemnation they live in because of their sin. The light has come into the world; but if people choose darkness instead of the light they will reap the harvest of their own foolishness. Those who do evil hate the light for fear that their deeds will be exposed. On the other hand, those who live by the truth come into the light, so that it may be seen plainly that what they do has been done through my grace.

Whether a person walks in the light or the darkness, then, will affect their eternal destiny. When giving the apostle John the revelation of heaven, Jesus told him that those who would be shut out of the Kingdom of heaven were those who had preferred the darkness to the light. Of course, as the Judge of the living and the dead, I, and I alone, determine what is darkness and what is light. Anything that does not agree with me and my word is darkness.

Outside the Kingdom of heaven are those who practice magic arts, those who indulge in occult practices. Also excluded are the sexually immoral, the adulterers, those who indulge in sexual acts outside marriage or in homosexual and lesbian relationships. There are many who belong to my Kingdom now who once indulged in such activities. They have had to repent, to seek forgiveness, to turn away from their sins and embrace my righteous purposes for their lives. Such practices do not belong in the lives of those who are part of my Kingdom.

Remember, beloved, it is sin you condemn, not sinners. You are to be a witness of my saving grace to those in darkness and to any brother or sister who sins; the sinner you want to see saved and embracing the life of my Kingdom, the brother or sister you desire to see restored to a life of faith and loving obedience.

Murderers and idolaters are also excluded. The worship of idols can save no one. Sadly, there are many who worship demonic spirits and live in fear of them. I don't call you to a religion of fear, but to a life of love.

Understand that an idol is anything or anyone who is worshipped, who is allowed to take my rightful place in a person's life. Those who worship me on earth will have the joy of worshipping me eternally in heaven.

Jesus also warns that those outside the Kingdom include those who practice falsehood, the deceivers, liars, cheats and perpetrators of corruption in its many forms. Do I not have the right to exclude from heaven those I know should have no place there? They will reap the harvest of unrighteousness they have sown.

Beloved, you will hear some argue that because I am the loving Father I would not exclude anyone from heaven. Do they think they know better than Jesus, who came from heaven?

I will not exclude any child of grace; but, whether they realize it or not, those outside my Kingdom have chosen the prince of darkness as their lord; he is their father. They worship him by the things they say and do.

Beloved child, this grieves me far more than it grieves you; for I have provided the way out of the darkness. **Don't judge them; love them and reach out to them with the light of my truth and love.** They need to be rescued; many don't realize the danger they are in!

1 Corinthians 6:9–10   Galatians 5:19–21   Colossians 3:5–6

76

Called by Grace

God, who has saved us and called us to a holy life – not because of anything we have done but because of his own purpose and grace.
2 Timothy 1:9

Beloved, some people criticize me for my gracious way of acting. 'Why should He choose some and not others?' they ask. It seems they are offended that not all are chosen. They forget that nobody *deserves* to be chosen, not one! Everyone who is forgiven is forgiven through my mercy and grace alone. Everyone who receives new life does so as a work of my grace. Everyone called to minister in my name does so by my grace. No one can live in Christ Jesus except by my grace. Nobody deserves anything!

It is my grace and kindness that leads any sinners to repentance and to the new life that I offer. Some remain stubborn in their refusal to repent. They hear the gospel of my grace, of my desire to give them my Kingdom, but they reject what I offer. They choose rather to be the lord of their lives instead of recognizing me as their Lord. They persist in their own lives of independence and refuse to submit to me, to my will or my ways. They refuse the offer of life I have given them. And they certainly don't want to be holy!

This is why Jesus says that many are called but few are chosen. Those who refuse my call reject my grace. I am willing to be gracious to any who turn to me in repentance and faith. Those who persist in their stubborn and unrepentant hearts are stirring up wrath for themselves. You see, my beloved, it is not that I am unwilling to be gracious to them, but they have rejected my grace.

I want all people everywhere to be saved! This is why I sent my Son to be their Saviour. You can see that those who reject the truth only have themselves to blame for their eventual destiny. It saddens me that any should reject my offer of life.

Consider what happened during Jesus' ministry. It was many of the religious leaders of the day who rejected the gospel of my grace and refused the life Jesus came to offer. Their security was in their traditions and their self-righteousness, instead of in Jesus and His righteousness. They were holy in their own eyes, but not in mine!

Yes, some were sincere. Many who reject the gospel are sincere. But sincerity doesn't give you eternal life; only faith in Jesus can do that. So some persist in deception or disobedience because they reject the One who came full of grace and truth.

I want everyone to hear the gospel. That is why I send all those who honour and love me out into the world with the great commission I have given to my Church, to make disciples of all nations. I don't want my Kingdom to be exclusive. Doesn't Jesus tell His followers to go out and compel people to come in because I want the heavenly banquet to be full? If those who are offered a place refuse, go and find others who will respond to the truth and become recipients of all I offer by my grace.

What about those who have never heard the gospel, have never come within sound of the truth? They are my business, not yours. You don't have to judge anyone. I alone am the Judge of the living and the dead. Your task, along with that of every other believer, is to make Jesus known, for there can be no doubt of the eternal destiny of those who are saved. All who are grateful that I have called and chosen them need to be available for me to use them to call others.

Understand this, beloved: I don't make it your responsibility to force people to respond to the gospel; but I want to use you to be a witness of the truth, to demonstrate the benefits of belonging to my Kingdom. And be thankful that you have been called and chosen, as a work of sheer grace on my part!

Because you are my holy child, I have set you apart to live in Christ, the Holy One, and to make Him known to others.

I revealed through my prophet Ezekiel that the nations will know that I am the Lord when I show myself holy through those who are my people. I therefore want to show myself holy through you. This is why I have set you apart. Don't be scared at what this will involve, for this will bring much joy into your life. It is the unholy things that cause you all the problems and put you at odds with me.

Mark 7:8–9   Mark 7:13   Luke 14:23

77

Your Ministry Is to Love

*I tell you the truth, whatever you did for one of the least
of these brothers of mine, you did for me.*
Matthew 25:40

My beloved, I have a ministry for everyone of my children. Your ministry is your service. I call you to serve others, and in serving them you serve me. Whatever you do to them you do to me.

You cannot love me unless you love others. You see, beloved, because you have a heart of love you are to love any who are around to love! Of course, you will love me first and foremost. You will love other family members. You will love your brothers and sisters in the local expression of my Body to which you belong. You will love those with whom you work. You will love those around you who have need. You will even love your enemies, those who oppose you in any way. In loving these people you will love me and so walk in agreement with me.

Yes, I have a distinctive ministry for each one of my children. Some I call to pastor, to care for the sheep. Others I send out into the world with compassion ministries, to show people my loving concern and care for them. They are my witnesses, reaching others with the practical outworking of the good news of the Kingdom.

Some I send out as evangelists. They have a boldness to confront people with the issues of the gospel, and an anointing to lead people to a point of decision so that they embrace the life of my Kingdom.

Even if you do not see yourself as a pastor or evangelist, I have my appointed ministry for you, beloved, for I have made you a witness. Your effectiveness in this is dependent not on your ability, but on your anointing. I want you to keep that anointing fresh upon your life, believing that I will use you powerfully and effectively. Don't think it is impossible for you to impact the lives of others in significant ways. My Spirit working through you can have a profound effect on others, sometimes without you realizing this is happening.

You only have to serve and love each one as I lead you, allowing me to speak and act through you. **Remember, I only have ordinary men and women through whom to work; and I am able to do extraordinary things through them!**

Consider for a moment my children who have had an impact on your life. It was not what they are in the natural that influenced you for good, but what I have made them and the way I worked through them to help, bless and encourage you. They did not think of themselves as mighty men and women of God, yet you will always be thankful for them.

If I can work through others to be a blessing to you, then I can work through you to bless others. Expect this.

One of the ways in which you can serve both them and me most effectively is through prayer. Yes, as you intercede for people my life and power can touch their lives to transform and heal them. For I answer prayer with my supernatural life that transcends anything you could do for them in the natural.

So be encouraged, beloved. You don't have to look for a ministry that will be recognized as such by other people. It doesn't have to be filled with the spectacular. Just get on with the business of loving and serving people in my name. Pray for them and expect that in some way my life and power will touch their lives. And be thankful for the ways in which I use you.

Romans 12:9–19   2 Corinthians 6:3–10   2 Corinthians 4:1–3

78

Grace for Ministry

I became a servant of this gospel by the gift of God's
grace given me through the working of his power.
Ephesians 3:7

Beloved, when I call my children to distinctive ministries they require distinctive grace. You don't need grace for things to which you are not called, but you certainly need grace for everything to which you are called!

To the apostle I give the anointing for that particular calling, the grace to be an apostle. This is why my servant Paul could appeal to the grace that was given him to exercise that distinctive office.

To the teacher I give the grace to teach, but not to be an apostle. Teachers don't need that distinctive apostolic grace, because that is not their calling nor what they are appointed to do in my name. However, they do need the grace to teach; so that is the grace I impart to them.

Evangelists have the grace they need to confront others with their need to repent and believe. And that grace enables them to be fruitful in their calling.

The grace that pastors need is often very different from that of the evangelist, for pastors are called to care, to build up and encourage those who have become my children, so each can be fruitful in their respective calling. They need my grace to be effective as pastors.

The prophet needs prophetic grace, the healer the grace to manifest my healing power for my glory. The administrator needs my grace to administrate effectively.

Beloved, it is apparent when someone is trying to do things without anointing and therefore without the necessary flow of grace that would enable them to be effective. I will always give my grace to enable my children to move in my will; but I will not grace them to do what I haven't called them to do. You can see how anointing and the grace to flow in that anointing belong together.

It is a blessing to hear someone preach or teach who is anointed to do so. You know my grace is at work as you listen to what is said, and you are blessed as a result. On the other hand, it can be a painful experience to hear someone preach who is not anointed to do so. My grace is not evident in such situations, and so people are not blessed in the same way.

What is true of preaching and teaching is also true in principle of all the ministry gifts. However, it is not enough to be anointed. The anointed need to flow in their anointing and not in the flesh. When they depend on me and the anointing I have given, then my grace abounds through what they do. But when they trust to themselves and not to the anointing, then they promote themselves, and there is no grace in that!

Beloved, I call you to the work of ministry, to serve and help others in my name. As you learn to depend on my grace, you will discover the particular ways in which my grace can work through you to enable you to be a blessing to others. Trust in my grace to cause you to have an effective ministry to others.

If I ask you to do something outside your normal scope of ministry, you can be sure that I will always give you the necessary grace to do what I ask. When you step out in faith to obey me, you will discover that I supply all the grace you need to accomplish successfully the task I place before you. Because you know you could not have accomplished those things through your own ability, you will give me all the glory. The secret is this: Christ in *you*!

Ephesians 4:11–13   1 John 2:20   1 John 2:27

79

I Will Make Your Way Perfect

It is God who arms me with strength and makes my way perfect.
Psalm 18:32

My beloved, here is a further challenge to your faith. You have never believed that I could make your way perfect! Even though I give you my power and make all the resources of my Spirit available, you are convinced you will inevitably fail to be the person I want you to be and to do all I ask of you. If your expectation is failure, you will surely fail. Because I am perfect I cannot do anything imperfect! Therefore every time you trust me to act, what I do will always be perfect.

I am the sure Rock on which you stand. When you trust me you will not falter. I enable you to rise spiritually above your circumstances, to exercise the faith and authority you have in Christ. I give you the shield of victory. I sustain you and make you great, so that your enemies flee before you. Even though you walk in the narrow way, I make the path broad beneath your feet and I keep you from stumbling. I make you an overcomer. I hear the cry of your heart and I answer you!

Does all this seem so unreal to you? It is my word, and I call you to live in agreement with my word! I don't say that *you* will make your way perfect. I will do this. I don't say that you in yourself will be perfect; but when you trust me, I will make your way perfect. This means that my will for you shall be accomplished, my promises fulfilled; that I will enable you to overcome. I will sustain you; I will broaden your feet and will prevent you from stumbling or falling. I will make you great.

Does this surprise you, that I want you to be great? Well, I do – in Kingdom terms. The greatest in the Kingdom are the greatest servants; they use the authority, power and life of my

Spirit to serve others. They demonstrate that my Kingdom is not a matter of talk, but of power. Are you learning the lesson, beloved? When you trust in yourself you fail, no matter how hard you try. When you yield yourself to me and trust me, I make your way perfect!

Do you not see how encouraging it is to read such scriptures as those I refer to? You need to do this every day, for my word will build you up and strengthen you in your faith. Spending time doing this is not a duty or a chore; it should be a delight, for everyone likes to be encouraged. However, this is more than a joy: it is a life-line.

Every day I will speak to you through my word, enabling you to see things as I see them! As you trust me to do what I promise, this takes the pressure away from you. As a child who is happy to serve, you only have to do what I ask of you with the authority, grace and encouragement I give, and you can trust me that the outcome will be good.

Remember, beloved, I have chosen good works for you to walk in: I will make your way perfect. And when you are under pressure from the enemy it is I who will come to rescue you and show you my unfailing love.

Hebrews 10:14   Matthew 5:48   1 Peter 1:15–16

Revival: A Life of Agreement

Then the nations will know that I am the LORD,
declares the Sovereign LORD, *when I show myself holy*
through you before their eyes.
Ezekiel 36:23

My beloved, faith is a matter of agreeing with me. Obedience is a matter of agreeing with me. Walking in the Spirit is a matter of agreeing with me. Speaking, acting and praying in my name is a matter of agreeing with me. This is what it means to abide in me and I in you, that you live in agreement with me.

Do you see what I intend for you, beloved? **I want you to be united with me in love, living in the agreement of faith so that you will speak, act and pray in my name with the authority I give you in the power of my Spirit.**

Agreement with me gives you great authority. In fact, you can only exercise spiritual authority to the degree in which you are submitted to my authority and are living in agreement with me. It is by the exercise of authority that you will see the evidence of my power working through you, and the fulfilment of the promises I have given you.

Jesus exercised the authority of the Holy One of God over all that is unholy. **I call my children to be a holy people so that they too may exercise my authority over an unholy world.**

Do you now understand holiness in its simplest terms? Yes, it is agreement with me.

- **What is faith? Agreement with me.**
- **What is obedience? Living in agreement with me.**
- **What does it mean to walk in the Spirit? To live in agreement with me.**

- **What is true repentance? Bringing your life into agreement with me and, therefore, with my will for you.**
- **What does it mean to say that I am Lord in your life? That you live in agreement with me.**
- **What does it mean to live the life of my Kingdom here on earth? To live in agreement with me.**
- **How will you see the fulfilment of all the prophetic words that have been spoken over your life? By living in agreement with me.**

You have the message. So, beloved, what are you going to do in response?

- **What is rebellion? Living in disagreement with me!**
- **What is independence? Disagreement with me.**
- **What is disobedience? Disagreement with me.**
- **What is sin in its many forms? Disagreement with me.**

So you have to choose. Either you set your heart on living in agreement with me, or you will inevitably live in disagreement.

When you make the right choice, you receive fresh revelation of my love, mercy and grace to enable you. I give you a fresh release of my Holy Spirit to empower you; a fresh release of my wisdom and prophetic clarity, so that you know the way in which I want you to walk. And I give you a fresh release of my authority to enable you to overcome the obstacles, authority to overcome whatever is in disagreement with me.

Beloved, do you want to live in revival? When in revival, my people live in agreement with me. This means they are living the life I always intended for my Church and all who are part of my Body on earth. I never intended my Church, or any of my children, to live in disagreement with me.

A people living in agreement with me will be able to impact the nations with my truth. Because they live the life of the Kingdom, I can use them to extend my Kingdom on earth significantly.

What kind of leaders do I want in my Church? Those who will give the example of living in agreement with me, and will teach and encourage others to do likewise. **Such leaders will produce a holy people, a people of faith, of love, of obedience, of authority and power. Because they live close to me, they will enable others to draw close to me.**

And what of you, my beloved child? Do you not perceive even more fully now how much I love you, that I should want to draw you closer to me, to live in closer agreement with me? Do you not see how much you matter to me and to the cause of my Kingdom, that I should want you to be in agreement with me? Do you not see the immense possibilities this opens to you?

Please don't look back over your past record. I am ready to forgive whatever needs to be forgiven in that regard. No, look forward in expectation that increasingly you are going to live in agreement with me.

This will bless me so much!

1 John 1:7   1 John 2:6   3 John 4